How to use Roth and IRA accounts to provide a secure retirement
2025 Edition

by

Michael Gray, CPA
with Thi T. Nguyen, CPA

ISBN 978-0-9794438-6-2

Copyright Notices

LEGAL NOTICES:

While all attempts have been made to provide effective, verifiable information in this book, neither the author nor publisher assumes any responsibility for errors, inaccuracies, or omissions. Any slights of people or organizations are unintentional.

If advice concerning tax, legal, compliance, or related matters is needed, the services of a qualified professional should be sought. This publication is designed to provide accurate and authoritative information in regard to the subject matter covered. It is sold with the understanding that the publisher is not engaged in rendering legal, accounting, or other professional service. If legal advice or other expert assistance is required, the services of a competent professional person should be sought.

Since federal and local laws differ widely, as do codes of conduct for members of professional organizations and agencies, the licensee must accept full responsibility for determining the legality and/or ethical character of any and all business transactions and/or practices adopted and enacted in his or her particular field and geographic location, whether or not those transactions and/or practices are suggested, either directly or indirectly, in this book.

As with any business advice, the reader is strongly encouraged to seek professional counsel before taking action. NOTE: No guarantees of savings or profits are intended by this book. Many variables affect each individual's results. Your results will vary from the examples given.

Michael Gray, CPA and Thi Nguyen, CPA have no control over what you may do or not do with this book, and therefore cannot accept the responsibility for your results. You are the only one who can initiate action in order to reap your own rewards!

You are hereby advised that any written tax advice contained in this communication was not written or intended to be used (and cannot be used) by any taxpayer for the purpose of avoiding penalties that may be imposed under the U.S. Internal Revenue Code.

Published by:
Silicon Valley Publishing Co.
2482 Wooding Ct.
San Jose, CA 95128-4271
United States of America
ISBN 978-0-9794438-6-2

For more information

For more information, write to Thi T. Nguyen, CPA, thi@atl-cpa.com.

Are you seeking a speaker for your group about IRAs and Roth IRAs? Are you seeking a resource for a story about IRAs and Roth IRAs?

Thi T. Nguyen, CPA is available for a limited number of presentations about IRAs and Roth IRAs and for media interviews. For more information, write Ms. Thi Nguyen, CPA at thi@atl-cpa.com.

For developments relating to IRAs and Roth IRAs in addition to other tax issues, subscribe to *Michael Gray, CPA's Tax and Business Insight* at no charge or obligation at www.taxtrimmers.com. Michael Gray also writes about tax developments at his blog, www.michaelgraycpa.com.

Gift Certificate

ATL CPAs & Advisors inc

Gift Certificate

ATL CPAs & Advisors, Inc.

AMOUNT : $275 VALID UNTIL : 12/31/2025

333 W. Santa Clara St., Ste. 620, San Jose, CA 95113
THI@ATL-CPA.COM

Praise for
How to use Roth and IRA accounts to provide a secure retirement

"Finally, a book on IRAs anyone can understand. Michael has done a great job of explaining how we all can retire and not count on Social Security. This little book contains the relevant facts about IRAs and eliminates the bible sized manuals written for CPAs. Well done."

Ron LeGrand
www.ronlegrand.com

"Do these two things now to create your secure retirement nest-egg (while avoiding debilitating tax traps): buy this book and start saving regularly."

Michael J. Jones, CPA
Thompson Jones LLP
www.thompsonjones.com

"How to use Roth and IRA Accounts to Provide a Secure Retirement is not sales propaganda published to help the broker "make the sale." It is an investor's working manual to take charge of the conversation in order to make decisions best suited for the saver of the capital to be invested. If you are an investor, you can use this book to know what is possible, why it is possible, and how to use an IRA and/or a Roth as a building block in your financial planning.

"I also recommend this book to anyone who is interviewing for a new financial advisor and would like to ask fact based questions and not be blinded with charts and graphs giving the company line. Use the information in the book to ask the potential advisor questions they should know before you give your money over for new management. Ask yourself, can a new advisor truly help me with what is possible when the advisor has not taken the time to learn about IRAs and Roths?"

Dick Blakeley
The Blakeley Group, Inc.
www.theblakeleygroup.com

"Many individuals have recently begun to discover the 'secret' of taking advantage of certain tax benefits to maximize the return on their retirement accounts. These plans, known as Individual Retirement Arrangements (IRAs), were initially authorized pursuant to the Employee Retirement Income Security Act (ERISA) when it was signed into law on Labor Day, 1974, so IRAs have been around for a while. However, relatively few individuals – accountants, lawyers, and financial planners among them – really understand how IRAs work and how they can be used to maximum advantage in retirement planning. After all, the regulations were created by both the Department of Labor and the Department of the Treasury, so some degree of complexity would be expected. Michael Gray, a Certified Public Accountant, has successfully compiled a practical overview of the key points of these regulations into a concise summary that anyone can use to learn the basics about this otherwise obscure retirement planning tool. Of course, you should consult with a knowledgeable financial planning, tax, and legal advisor before making any investment choices. But reading Michael Gray's book will put you well ahead of the curve in your ability to ask the right questions and make intelligent financial decisions for your retirement."

Jeffrey B. Hare, Attorney at Law
jeff@jeffreyhare.com

"The world of retirement accounts can be complex and mysterious to the average investor or retirement saver. This work by Michael Gray simplifies much of the jargon and complex rules. As such, the typical consumer can learn and take advantage of the positive aspects of savings vehicles, in particular, the Roth IRA that is probably the best U.S. savings vehicle ever created. Thirty per cent of the graying U.S. population has no retirement savings, and most others are insufficiently prepared. It is critical to the development of a sound private retirement system, that comprehensive and understandable educational information like Michael Gray's reach the public so that a renewed interest in saving is stimulated!"

Tom W. Anderson
President, Retirement Industry Trust Association (RITA) and
Founder and Vice Chairman
PENSCO Trust Company
www.PENSCO.com

"The book is great. It is an excellent summary of some very complex law. I love the section on Roth vs Traditional IRAs. It is the best summary explanation I have seen on the subject."

Raymond Sheffield, Esq.
Sheffield Law Office
www.sheffieldestateplanning.com

"I have known Michael Gray, CPA for most of the 35 years I have been in the financial planning and asset management business. Some of our clients are also served by Michael Gray for tax consulting and tax return preparation services. In my opinion, Mike's clients are getting a bargain in having his professional expertise available! This new book represents a practical guide to IRA and Roth IRA decision making for the average investor. As a professional in the financial industry, I consider this book to be an invaluable resource for my desk."

Craig Martin, MSFS, CFP, CLU, ChFC
Fee-only financial planner
The Family Wealth Consulting Group
www.fwcg.net

Contents

Copyright Notices 2
For more information 3
Gift Certificate 4
Praise for *How to use Roth and IRA accounts to provide a secure retirement* 5
1 Introduction 8
2 Why a Roth or IRA is a key element in a retirement plan 10
3 Roth or IRA? 12
4 Single-person 401(k) and SEP alternatives for the Self-Employed 19
5 What kinds of investments can you make with a Roth or IRA? 25
6 Look before you leap! Due diligence 28
7 What kinds of transactions must you avoid with your Roth or IRA? (Prohibited transactions.) 36
8 Making alternative investments in a Roth or IRA using a self-directed account 40
9 A case study 43
10 When Roths and IRAs owe income taxes – The Unrelated Business Income Tax 46
11 Where to get help with your investments 49
12 Creating a bigger account – rollovers from qualified plans (401(k)s) 50
13 Converting a tax deferred account to a tax-free account – at a price (Roth conversions) 52
14 What distributions can you take from a Roth or IRA before age 59 ½? 56
15 Distributions permitted from a Roth or IRA starting age 59 ½ and before the required beginning date 61
16 Required annual distributions during the participant's lifetime after the required beginning date 62
17 Valuation and retirement accounts 66
18 Estate Planning for IRAs and Roths 69
19 Handling an IRA or Roth account after a death 83
20 Divorce 92
21 Additional references 94
22 About the Authors 97
Appendix A Retirement Plan Calendar checklist for after a death 99
Appendix B IRS Actuarial Tables for Distributions 104

1
Introduction

The most significant assets of most individuals in the United States are their home and their retirement account. (High tech executives also have employee stock options, real estate investors have their real estate and other investors have their securities accounts.)

Financing a retirement can be challenging. Life expectancy keeps getting longer. According to the Society of Actuaries, there is a 74% chance that one of a married couple age 65 will live to age 90 and a 46% chance that one of them will live to age 95.[1] That's a long time!

Baby boomers are in or approaching their retirement years. They face difficult choices about what to do with their 401(k) accounts. Should they leave them with the plan or roll them over to an IRA?

(In this book, a "Roth" account is a Roth IRA account and an "IRA" account is a regular/traditional IRA or individual retirement account. An "employer plan" is a qualified retirement plan relating to your employment, including 401(k), profit sharing, 403(b) for nonprofit, 457 for government, and other less common plans. Employer plans are critically important and beyond the scope of this book. Please consult with a tax advisor who is familiar with them for your employer plan accounts.)

During a participant's lifetime, he or she can now convert a "regular" IRA to a Roth account. In addition, some "regular" 401(k) accounts can be converted to Roth 401(k) accounts. The SECURE 2.0 Act of 2022 made even more employer retirement plans eligible to have designated Roth accounts, including permitting employer contributions to those accounts.

Participants in retirement plans should find out if their retirement plan offers Roth options and seriously consider electing to make Roth conversions of part or all of their retirement account balances and having future contributions, including employer contributions, be Roth contributions. Since this election makes more income currently taxable, tax projections should be made to avoid underpayments of estimated taxes and to avoid a cash bind creating financial distress. Plan this carefully with your tax advisor.

In this book, I intend to provide a framework for further discussion with your tax and investment advisors. I have written the book for the layperson. This is not an exhaustive, technical explanation.

I intentionally haven't extensively documented the text. The footnote references are for convenience when questions come up.

---

1 American Academy of Actuaries and Society of Actuaries, Actuaries Longevity Illustrator, http://www.longevityillustrator.org/, accessed February 8, 2023.

The detailed rules and choices have grown to be staggering, so I am intentionally focusing on the highlights to provide an overview. If you believe I have missed a significant area that should be included, please write to me at mgray@taxtrimmers.com and I'll consider including it in later editions of this book.

Remember to check for the state tax consequences of your transaction. Many states have tax rules that don't conform to the Internal Revenue Code. For example, California taxes long-term capital gains at the same tax rates as ordinary income.

Whenever we write about tax laws, we have a moving target. Tax laws change regularly, including new rulings by the courts and the IRS, new Treasury Regulations, and new tax laws passed by Congress. Most recently, the IRS issued final and proposed regulations for required minimum distributions from IRAs and employer retirement plans, published in the Federal Register on July 19, 2024. The SECURE 2.0 Act of 2022 was enacted on December 29, 2022. Significant relief provisions were included in the Coronavirus Aid, Relief and Economic Security Act of 2020 or "CARES Act". Additional changes for retirement and inherited retirement accounts were included in the Setting Every Community Up for Retirement Enhancement Act of 2019 or "SECURE Act." Investors should consult with tax advisors about these matters. Tax advisors must be alert for developments and perform research to support their advice. One way to keep up to date is to subscribe to *Michael Gray, CPA's Tax and Business Insight* at www.taxtrimmers.com. Until further notice, there is no charge or obligation to subscribe to this email newsletter.

A big "Thank you!" to the folks who read preliminary versions of this book and gave me suggestions to improve it. Thi Nguyen, CPA with ATL CPA & Advisors, Inc., who is the successor for my former tax consulting and tax return preparation practice, is a contributor. Michael Jones, CPA with Thompson Jones LLP has awesome technical expertise in the tax laws relating to IRAs, Roths and estate planning, so I was especially delighted that he agreed to read the text for previous editions and gave extensive suggestions. He opted out of reviewing the 2025 Edition. Financial planner Dick Blakeley gave suggestions. Lori Greymont, Chief Executive Officer of the San Jose Real Estate Investors Association volunteered to contribute material about due diligence for the book. Tom Anderson, founder of PENSCO Trust Company and President of the Retirement Industry Trust Association (RITA), has a wealth of hands-on experience from which he made many valuable suggestions. Other friends who generously read the book with feedback included Ron LeGrand, Craig Martin, Naomi Comfort, Lamaar Baxter, Jeffrey Hare and Raymond Sheffield.

Natalie Choate, author of *Life and Death Planning for Retirement Benefits,* generously answered some questions as I worked on this book. Her book and update material at www.ataxplan.com, were invaluable resources.

You have a much more valuable resource in your hands thanks to their contributions.

Enjoy!

Michael Gray, CPA
October 22, 2024

2

Why a Roth or IRA is a key element in a retirement plan

Since they were introduced back in 1974, individual retirement accounts have become very significant in retirement planning. The addition of the Roth individual retirement account in 1998 and the extension of designated Roth accounts to most employer plans by the SECURE 2.0 Act of 2022 have provided additional important items to the retirement planning menu.

Social Security is under growing pressure because we have an aging population, including an enormous "bubble" of retirements to be funded for the "baby boom" generation. (I'm a member!) I think the likely resolution of the Social Security dilemma will be to raise the retirement age when we are eligible for full benefits. Time will tell. Social Security is a cornerstone of the U.S. retirement system and I don't see our government allowing it to become bankrupt or severely curtailing it. (The AARP won't let them!)

The U.S. government knows it can't provide a comfortable retirement for all of us, so it must encourage and subsidize private solutions. That's why we have tax incentives for employer-provided and personal (Roth and traditional IRA) retirement plans.

Principally resulting from relief measures for natural disasters and the COVID-19 pandemic, a huge military budget to fund overseas military operations, funding health care reform, and the tax cuts in the Tax Cuts and Jobs Act of 2017, the U.S. government is incurring record deficits, which it seems must eventually lead to higher taxes to repay.

Effective for tax years after 2017 and scheduled to expire after 2025, the maximum federal income tax rate is 37%. An additional 3.8% tax on net investment income has been added to the mix as part of health care reform. (Mercifully, the net investment income tax doesn't apply to taxable income from a qualified retirement plan or an IRA.)

The reduction of federal income tax rates under the Tax Cuts and Jobs Act of 2017 means income taxes are currently "on sale." As I write this, both Presidential candidates are promising extension of the tax cuts, at least for married taxpayers with income of $400,000 or less. Although this seems to reduce the incentives for sheltering income in retirement accounts, the tax cuts may not be sustainable, so it makes sense to take advantage of tax-favored retirement vehicles. With the Jobs Act provisions expiring after 2025, Congress will certainly be arguing about tax law extensions and changes during 2025.

The premise of an IRA and most tax-deferred retirement accounts is to postpone subjecting income to tax until retirement, when you will probably be in a lower tax bracket. Many high-income taxpayers have found that they continue to be in high tax brackets after retirement, so the premise doesn't work for them unless they can shift the funds to low-bracket family members after death or to a charity. By converting to a Roth account now, they can pay tax at lower tax rates and escape tax on future earnings and growth in the account. Converting traditional retirement accounts to Roth accounts also eliminates many of the problems for inherited retirement accounts, because distributions from Roth accounts are tax-free. The problem is finding the cash to pay income taxes for the conversion.

By the way, the Roth account is no accident. Converting a taxable retirement account to a Roth IRA was a way for the U.S. government to accelerate tax revenues.

In summary, U.S. tax rates will probably increase as the federal and state governments continue to look for additional revenue sources. When providing for a long-term obligation, like funding your retirement, using a tax-free Roth account can be a great advantage.

Depending on your tax picture, traditional/regular IRA accounts also have tax advantages because of the up-front tax deduction for traditional IRA accounts and the ability to grow your investments, usually without paying a current tax, and having a bigger fund to work with gives you more choices of investments to make.

For taxpayers in lower tax brackets, the "saver's credit" is an additional incentive for saving using a Roth or IRA. The credit is up to 50% of a contribution of up to $2,000 (for a maximum $1,000 credit) to certain retirement accounts, including regular IRAs, Roth IRAs, 401(k)s, 403(b) annuities, a governmental 457 plan, a SIMPLE IRA, a salary reduction SEP or an ABLE account. The percentage of the retirement plan contribution for which a credit is allowed is reduced until the credit is eliminated for married taxpayers filing joint returns for 2024 with adjusted gross income (AGI) exceeding $76,500, heads of household with AGI exceeding $57,375, and all others with AGI exceeding $38,250. For 2025, the thresholds are married taxpayers filing joint returns with AGI exceeding $79,000, heads of household with AGI exceeding $59,250, and all others with AGI exceeding $3,500. In order to claim the credit, you must be at least 18 years old, you may not be a full-time student, and no one else may claim your personal exemption. See Publication 4703 and Form 8880 at the IRS web site, www.irs.gov.

Effective for taxable years ending after December 31, 2026, the "saver's credit" will be changed to a "saver's match." The "match" is a cash federal matching contribution to be deposited to the taxpayer's IRA or retirement account of up to 50% of the taxpayer's IRA or retirement plan contributions to a maximum of $2,000. The "match" applies to contributions to certain retirement accounts, including regular IRAs, Roth IRAs, 401(k) s, 403(b) annuities, a governmental 457 plan, a SIMPLE IRA, a salary reduction SEP or an ABLE account. The percentage of the retirement plan contribution for which a match is allowed is reduced until the match is eliminated for married taxpayers filing joint returns with adjusted gross income (AGI) from $41,000 to $71,000, heads of household with AGI from $30,750 to $53,250, and all others with AGI from $20,500 to $35,500. In order to claim the credit, you must be at least 18 years old, you may not be a full-time student, and no one else may claim your personal exemption.

These benefits make Roths and traditional IRAs key elements of your retirement planning toolkit.

3

Roth or Traditional IRA?

The title of this chapter is a trick question.

Probably over a lifetime you will need to use both a Roth and a traditional IRA.

Rules of thumb

Instead of keeping you in suspense, I'll give you some rules of thumb up front. The right decisions for you will very much depend on your individual circumstances, so I recommend that you seek help from a financial planner and/or tax consultant when making decisions relating to retirement accounts.

1 The younger you are, the more a Roth is favored. You will have more time to accumulate a bigger retirement fund through untaxed compound earnings during your lifetime and the lifetime of a surviving spouse successor. (The ability of beneficiaries to spread the distribution of an inherited Roth account income tax free over their life expectancies has mostly been eliminated by the SECURE Act of 2020 and Treasury Regulations.)

2 If you expect your marginal tax bracket to go up, a Roth is favored. It's generally better to pay taxes at lower tax brackets. (This is a big wild card. Nobody really knows what our tax system will look like in the distant future, when many people will retire.)

3 If the beneficiary for the account is a charity, a traditional IRA is favored. Charities don't pay income taxes on retirement account proceeds. You might as well get a tax deduction for the money going into a retirement account if it's ultimately going to a charity. (Choosing which assets to give to a charity is an important part of estate planning. Assets that carry ordinary income, like retirement accounts and stock options, are good choices for charitable bequests.)

4 The more other assets that you have, the more a Roth is favored. Minimum distributions aren't required for a Roth during the lifetime of the account owner and when his or her spouse elects to roll over the account when it's inherited to his or her own account, during the lifetime of the surviving spouse. If you don't need the money, you can continue to accumulate earnings tax-free for a longer time than for a regular IRA. Minimum distributions are required from traditional IRAs starting on April 1 of the year after account owners reach their *applicable age.* See the explanations about the applicable age, required beginning date (RBD) and required minimum distributions in Chapter 16.

5 Not having a tax deduction for a contribution to a Roth or paying a tax for a conversion to a Roth can result in a financial hardship if you don't have the cash to pay the income taxes.

6 If you have beneficiaries who are individuals that you care about providing for, a Roth is generally favored because the Roth benefit isn't taxable. Charitable beneficiaries can also benefit from Roth accounts that don't have required minimum distributions during the account owner's lifetime.

7 If your beneficiaries are in higher tax brackets than you are, a Roth is favored. If you left them a taxable IRA account, they would have to pay more income taxes for distributions than you would.

Features, advantages and disadvantages of "regular"/"traditional" IRAs

Traditional individual retirement accounts or IRAs have been with us since the 1970s.

The maximum contribution is adjusted each year for inflation. For 2024, a taxpayer may contribute the lesser of $7,000 or his or her earned income each year to the IRA. In addition, taxpayers who are age 50 or older may contribute an additional $1,000 "catch up" contribution each year. The $1,000 "catch-up" contribution is also adjusted for inflation effective for taxable years beginning after December 31, 2023, and remains $1,000 for 2024. The $7,000 and $1,000 limits are unchanged for 2025. The contribution may be made up to the original due date for the tax year, usually April 15 of the year following the tax year.

A non-working spouse may also contribute to an IRA based on the earnings of the working spouse. Separate IRAs must be set up for each spouse.

The contribution may be deductible or non-deductible. The taxpayer may simply designate that he or she is making a non-deductible contribution.

The deduction is phased out for active participants in qualified retirement accounts and for their nonworking spouses. Despite the elimination of the deduction, nondeductible contributions can still be made up to the limitation listed above less any deductible contribution that is made and allowed.

An individual is an active participant who is covered by:

1 A qualified pension, profit sharing or stock bonus plan, including 401(k)s and ESOPs;

2 A qualified (employer provided) annuity plan;

3 A tax-sheltered annuity plan (for public employees);

4 A simplified employee pension (SEP);

5 A SIMPLE plan (small business 401(k) equivalent);

6 A plan established by the United States, a state or political subdivision of a state, or by a federal or state instrumentality; or

7 An employee-only contributory plan that is exempt from tax under Internal Revenue Code Section 501(c)(18).

For 2024, the deduction is phased out for active participant taxpayers who have adjusted gross income (before the IRA deduction) of $77,000 to $87,000 for single persons and heads of household and $123,000 to $143,000 for married persons filing a joint return. For 2025, the deduction is phased out for active participant taxpayers who have adjusted gross income (before the IRA deduction) of $79,000 to $89,000 for single persons and heads of household and $126,000 to $146,000 for married persons filing a joint return. No tax deduction is allowed for a contribution to an IRA for an active participant in an employer retirement plan who is a married person filing a separate income tax return.

For 2024, the deduction is phased out for nonworking spouses who are married to active participants with adjusted gross income (before the IRA deduction) from $230,000 to $240,000 on a married, filing a joint return. For 2025, the deduction is phased out for nonworking spouses who are married to active participants with adjusted gross income (before the IRA deduction) from $236,000 to $246,000 on a married, filing a joint return.

Non-deductible contributions are reported using Form 8606. The form is cumulative, tracking non-deductible contributions for the current and previous years.

A contribution to an IRA that exceeds the contribution limit is called an excess contribution. An excess contribution is subject to a cumulative, nondeductible 6% excess contribution tax. The tax applies every year until the year when the excess contribution is withdrawn from the IRA. The tax can be avoided by withdrawing the excess contribution plus any earnings on the contribution on or before the due date (including extensions) of the individual income tax return. (This is generally October 15 of the year following the year that the contribution relates to.)

The main advantage of a "regular" IRA is the tax benefit of the tax deduction for contributions helps to fund the account. For example, if you are in the 40% marginal tax bracket (you would pay 40% federal and state taxes combined on the next dollar earned), you would receive a tax benefit from a $7,000 deductible IRA contribution of $2,800. So, your tax savings are providing $2,800 of the amount contributed and you are providing the other $4,200.

A second advantage of a "regular" IRA is the tax deferral (in general) for earnings and any amounts rolled over from a taxable retirement account. The account can be a "parking" place for amounts received from an employer retirement account (usually a 401(k) account) when you terminate employment. This feature lets you accumulate additional capital and gives you more alternatives for investments to make with the account.

A third advantage of "regular" IRAs is you have control of the investments that you make, and may have more and better choices than are available in an employer plan. In many cases, an employer plan will simply offer a family of funds from a mutual fund company. They might not be the funds that you would choose. With the exception of a few prohibited investments, your choices with IRAs are virtually unlimited. Some investment companies offer self-directed accounts (for higher fees) that can give you this flexibility.

A nondeductible contribution to a regular IRA might provide a way to bypass the Roth contribution limit, since a traditional IRA may be converted to a Roth IRA. This is popularly known as a "backdoor Roth contribution." For this tax planning move to work, the regular IRA can't include any tax-deducted contributions or earnings on those amounts. (All IRAs are treated as one for this test.) On the other hand, it may be worthwhile making a "backdoor Roth contribution, even though you have to pay some income taxes, since future earnings in the Roth account will be income tax free.

Despite rumors that Congress might outlaw backdoor Roth contributions, they are still available after the enactment of SECURE 2.0.

A nondeductible contribution also provides the tax deferral feature like a regular IRA, but only on investment returns.

For those who are charitably inclined, a taxable IRA is an excellent choice of asset for a contribution. Normally, the only way to avoid a tax effect from making a donation from the account is to make the charity a beneficiary of the account. During your lifetime, you can have the funds as a contingency account to provide for your retirement or other needs, like long-term care.

A taxpayer age 70 ½ or older may make a qualified charitable distribution from a traditional IRA or Roth IRA. The distribution is not includable in taxable gross income of the taxpayer. No tax deduction is allowed for the charitable contribution. The maximum distribution amount is $105,000 for 2024 and $108,000 for 2025. (SEP IRAs and SIMPLE IRAs don't qualify for these distributions. These accounts can be rolled over to a regular IRA to avoid the exception.) The charitable distribution "counts" for meeting the required minimum distribution requirement.

The amount of qualified charitable distributions that are not includable in gross income is reduced by (1) the total amount of IRA deductions allowed to the taxpayer for all tax years ending on or after the date the taxpayer attains age 70 ½ minus (2) the total amount of reductions for qualified charitable distributions for all tax years preceding the current tax year. This was a compensating provision for IRA deductions becoming allowed on or after the year a taxpayer reached age 70 ½ under the SECURE Act of 2019.

For example, a taxpayer reached age 70 ½ during 2022. The taxpayer deducted IRA contributions of $6,000 for 2022, $6,500 for 2023 and $0 for 2024. The taxpayer made qualified charitable distributions of $0 for 2022, $6,000 for 2023 and $8,000 for 2024. For 2022, there was no qualified charitable distribution to reduce. For 2023, the exclusion is reduced by $12,500, the excess for IRA deductions for 2022 and 2023 minus $0 previous qualified charitable distributions, so all of the 2023 distribution will be taxable income. For 2024, the exclusion for the $8,000 distribution is reduced by the unused excess of the IRA deductions from 2023, $12,500 - $6,000 = $6,500, resulting in a $1,500 exclusion, so $1,500 of the 2024 distribution will be taxable income.

When a taxpayer makes substantial qualified charitable distributions, the reduction shouldn't be an issue. It will reduce the tax benefit of smaller distributions.

Effective for taxable years beginning after December 31, 2023 the $100,000 limitation for distributions by an IRA to a charity is indexed for inflation.[2] The adjusted limitation for 2024 is $105,000 and $108,000 for 2025.

Effective for taxable years ending after December 29, 2022, the charitable contribution exception for required minimum distribution includes up to a one-time $50,000 distribution to charities through charitable gift annuities, charitable remainder unitrusts, and charitable remainder annuity trusts. Since the trust may only be funded with this contribution, the administrative costs of maintaining them is likely to make this charitable vehicle impractical. This may be a "foot in the door" for increases by future tax law changes.

Some states don't recognize the exclusion for IRA distributions made directly to a charity. Check your local rules.

See Chapter 16 for the details about the age at which required minimum distributions must begin.

Despite increases in the required beginning date, taxpayers may still elect to contribute distributions to a qualified charity starting with the year they reach age 70 ½ "as if" the required minimum distribution requirements applied. However, if tax deductible IRA contributions were made in the year of the qualified charitable distribution, the qualified charitable distribution is included in gross income up to the amount of the IRA contributions. In that case, a charitable deduction must be claimed, and the net result may mean paying some income taxes on that distribution.

As a COVID-19 relief measure, the CARES Act suspended required minimum distributions for 2020. Taxpayers could still elect to contribute distributions to a qualified charity "as if" the required minimum distribution requirements applied.

Why is the lifetime gift to a charity an advantage? You bypass the 60% of adjusted gross income limit for charitable contributions that applies for tax years beginning after December 31, 2017 and before January 1, 2026. (Under the CARES Act, the charitable contributions limit was 100% of adjusted gross income for 2020.) You reduce your taxable estate and the charity gets the cash sooner.

A disadvantage of an IRA is a distribution (other than to a charity) carries taxable income.

Another disadvantage is IRAs must make required minimum distributions, as explained above and Chapter 16. Some people don't need this taxable income.

IRAs have a disadvantage relating to required distributions after the death of a participant who died after the required beginning date. See Chapters 16 and 19.

---

2 Internal Revenue Code § 408(d)(8)(G)

Features, advantages and disadvantages of Roth IRA accounts.

Roth accounts were enacted in 1998. They were developed to provide another retirement planning alternative in light of the challenges for Social Security. Since there is no deduction for contributions to a Roth account, there isn't an up-front tax receipts reduction to the U.S. Treasury. Tax revenue can also be generated by conversions of regular IRA and 401(k) accounts to Roth accounts. However, the long-term benefits can be significant.

For 2024, a taxpayer may contribute the lesser of $7,000 or his or her earned income to a Roth IRA. In addition, taxpayers who are age 50 or older may contribute an additional $1,000 "catch up" contribution each year. The $1,000 "catch-up" contribution is adjusted for inflation effective for taxable years beginning after December 31, 2023. The limit for 2024 is $1,000. The $7,000 and $1,000 limits are unchanged for 2025. The contribution may be made up to the original due date for the tax year, usually April 15 of the year following the tax year.

A non-working spouse may also contribute to a Roth IRA based on the earnings of his or her working spouse. Separate Roth IRAs must be set up for each spouse.

The maximum contribution is adjusted each year for inflation.

Unlike regular IRA contributions, Roth contributions are allowed even when you are covered by a qualified plan at work. The contribution limit is phased out based on adjusted gross income. For 2024, the maximum contribution is phased out for single persons for modified adjusted gross income between $146,000 and $161,000. For married persons filing joint returns, the maximum contribution is phased out for modified adjusted gross income between $230,000 and $240,000. For 2025, the maximum contribution is phased out for single persons for modified adjusted gross income between $150,000 and $165,000. For married persons filing joint returns, the maximum contribution is phased out for modified adjusted gross income between $236,000 and $246,000.

After meeting a five-year holding period requirement, distributions from Roth IRAs are tax-free, provided they also meet one of the following requirements:

1. Made on or after the date on which the participant reaches age 59 ½;
2. Made to a beneficiary (or the participant's spouse) after the participant's death;
3. Made to a disabled participant; or
4. Used to pay up to $10,000 (lifetime limit) of "qualified first-time homebuyer expenses."

A big advantage of Roth IRAs is distributions aren't required to be made during the lifetime of the participant. (Distributions are required after the death of the participant.) That means income can be accumulated in the accounts throughout the life of the participant for tax-free distribution to beneficiaries after the death of the participant.

A former advantage of Roth IRAs was repealed by the SECURE Act. Previously, taxpayers who reached age 70 ½ or older couldn't contribute to an IRA but could contribute to a Roth. Under the SECURE Act, taxpayers who are over the applicable age for required minimum distributions, age 75 for account owners of a traditional IRA who first reach age

74 after December 31, 2032, 73 for account owners who first reach age 72 after December 31, 2022 and age 73 before January 1, 2033, 72 for account owners who first reach age 70 1/2 after December 31, 2019 and age 72 before January 1, 2023, and 70 ½ for account owners who first reach age 70 ½ before 2020, can now continue contributing to either a Roth IRA or to a regular IRA.

Effective for distributions after December 31, 2023, Section 529 College Savings plans may rollover up to $35,000 over the course of a beneficiary's lifetime to the beneficiary's Roth IRA account. The 529 account must have been open for more than 15 years, and the rollover is limited to the annual Roth IRA contribution limit. The rollover also reduces other Roth IRA contributions for the rollover year. (As an alternative, consider rolling over the 529 account to another 529 account for a different member of the designated beneficiary's family.)

The rules for inherited retirement accounts, including Roth accounts, were significantly changed by the SECURE Act of 2019. See Chapter 19. Distributions from an inherited Roth account are tax free. Distributions from a regular IRA account are taxable or at least partially taxable (less any nondeductible contributions by the account owner).

The IRS has issued final Treasury Regulations to implement the SECURE Act of 2019. Since a Roth account doesn't have a required beginning date and a regular IRA does, beneficiaries receiving a Roth account after a participant's death can wait up to 10 years before distributing the account, giving the account additional time to grow *tax free.* (See Chapter 19 for an exception for eligible designated beneficiaries.) If there is no designated beneficiary, the limit is 5 years. Beneficiaries receiving a regular IRA after the death of a participant who dies after the required beginning date generally must receive life expectancy distributions during the first nine years after the participant's death and the balance of the account on the tenth year after death. See Chapters 16 and 19 for details.

The myRA – a discontinued Roth choice

President Obama initiated the myRA by executive order on January 29, 2014. On July 28, 2017, the IRS announced the myRA program was discontinued. MyRA owners are encouraged to roll their myRA accounts to regular Roth IRA accounts.

The purpose of the myRA was to enable small-dollar savers to establish a Roth IRA with a Treasury-designated custodian without paying fees or start-up costs. Participants could keep their myRA account and continue to make contributions when they changed jobs. The contribution limit was the same as for a regular Roth IRA account. Contributions to a myRA are invested in the Government Securities Investment Fund ("G Fund") previously available only to federal employees participating in a Thrift Savings Plan. Only individuals who are otherwise eligible to contribute to a Roth IRA may participate. Individuals could participate in a myRA until the sooner of when the total value of the myRA savings bond reached $15,000 or 30 years of participation. The account can be rolled over at any time to a regular Roth IRA account with a commercial financial services provider.[3]

The myRA was an attractive way to get started in accumulating a Roth account with a better interest rate than a conventional bank savings account.

3 RIN 1530-AA08, December 19, 2014

4

Single-person 401(k) and SEP alternatives for the Self-Employed

You will have the most investment choices if you have a large balance in your retirement account. For self-employed persons, single-person 401(k)s and Simplified Employee Pensions (SEPs) are retirement plan alternatives with the fewest compliance requirements. With these plans, self-employed persons (and their employees) can have self-directed accounts with minimal fiduciary duties.

The SECURE 2.0 Act of 2022 gave employers the option to amend their retirement plans to make the employer contribution to employee retirement accounts Roth contributions, or include this option when adopting a new retirement plan. Since distributions from Roth accounts aren't taxable and distributions aren't required from a Roth account during the employee's lifetime, employers should seriously consider adopting this option and employees should seriously consider electing employer contributions to a Roth account.

Single-person 401(k)s

Single-person 401(k)s can be contributed to like any other 401(k) plan, but have fewer compliance requirements. Since the compliance requirements are simpler, more custodians, including families of mutual funds and self-directed plan custodians, are willing to accept these plans compared to other qualified retirement plans.

The only participants of a single-person 401(k) can be the business owner and the business owner's spouse, and a partner and the partner's spouse.[4] If other employees are hired that are required to be covered by the plan, a single-person 401(k) plan will automatically convert to a regular 401(k) plan. Employees are generally "counted" when the employee is at least age 21 and has completed one year of service (works more than 1,000 hours in a plan year). Employees covered by a collective bargaining agreement can be excluded from a 401(k) plan covering other employees.

401(k) plans that aren't single person plans can be subject to testing for non-discrimination or being "top-heavy." Alternatively, the plan can require a 3% of compensation minimum employer contribution each year to eliminate the testing requirements. These requirements raise the cost of maintaining the plan.

Single-person plans with balances of less than $250,000 also aren't required to file the annual report, Form 5500, easing the compliance burden.

4 Internal Revenue Code § 401(a)(35)(E)(iv)

The maximum inflation-adjusted "employee" contribution for a 401(k) plan for 2024 is $23,000 and $23,500 for 2025, limited to 100% of compensation. An annual "catch up" contribution of up to $7,500 can also be made for 2024 for participants who are age 50 or older.

Effective for taxable years beginning after December 31, 2024, the catch-up limit for participants who attain ages 60, 61, 62 and 63 during the taxable year is increased to the greater of $10,000 or 50% more than the regular catch-up amount. The increased amounts will be indexed for inflation after 2025.

Effective for taxable years beginning after December 31, 2023, all catch-up contributions to 401(k), 403(b) and 457(b) qualified plans are subject to Roth tax treatment, except for catch-up contributions for employees with compensation of $145,000 or less, indexed for inflation after 2024. The threshold is unchanged at $145,000 for 2025. (That means those catch-up contributions won't be tax-deductible but the earnings on the contributions in the account generally won't be taxable when distributed to the participant or beneficiary.)

The IRS has announced administrative relief that makes Roth treatment of those catch-up contributions optional for employers for the first two taxable years beginning after December 31, 2023.[5]

Since employee contributions are withheld from compensation, they are made during the taxable year as wages are received and can't be made after the year-end. Effective for plan years beginning after December 29, 2022, the employee contribution *for the first year only* of a single-member 401(k) sponsored by a sole proprietor or a single-member LLC may be made by the due date for the owner's income tax return, without extensions (generally April 15 of the next year).

The employer contribution must be deposited no later than the extended due date of the owner's income tax return, provided an extension is timely filed (generally October 15 of the next year for individuals and calendar-year corporations; and September 15 for calendar-year S corporations and partnerships).

401(k)s can also have a "profit sharing" feature, permitting larger contributions than the amounts employees can usually elect to make. The maximum contribution (including both the "employer" and "employee" contributions) for 2024 is $69,000, and $70,000 for 2025, limited to 100% of compensation, net of retirement plan deferrals.

The "employee" contribution can be designated as a non-deductible Roth contribution. The Roth portion of the account needs to be accounted for separately in order to determine how much is eventually eligible for a tax-free distribution. See Chapter 13 on Roth conversions relating to "in plan" Roth conversions in 401(k) plans after September 25, 2010.

In the past, the "employer" contribution (including matching contributions) wasn't eligible for Roth treatment. Effective for contributions made after December 29, 2022, participants have the option for employer matching contributions and/or nonelective contributions to be made on a Roth basis. These contributions are currently taxable to the employee and are fully vested. The employer plan must be amended to accept employer

5 Notice 2023-62

Roth contributions before making such contributions.

This change eliminates the need for most "mega-backdoor Roth conversions." (Beyond the scope of this explanation.) Contributions to Roth accounts in employer retirement plans aren't subject to an income ceiling like contributions to Roth IRA accounts.

The employer's retirement plan reports any employer Roth contributions on behalf of an employee as a taxable distribution on Form 1099R. The amount is reported as income for the employee for the year the employer pays the contribution, not the year that the contribution relates to, so it may result in a one-year tax deferral of the taxable amount. The employer takes the tax deduction for the taxable year the contribution relates to, so there is a mismatch for the tax years of income and deduction for the employer and the employee. The employee's taxable income relating to the employer contribution isn't subject to income tax withholding or other payroll taxes, since it isn't paid to the employee. The employee should adjust his or her withholding or make estimated tax payments to avoid penalties for underpayment of estimated tax.[6]

Participant loans can be permitted from self-employed 401(k) plans, but I recommend that you avoid them. It's too easy to miss a compliance requirement, resulting in an unintentional distribution.

Also see Chapter 7 on prohibited transactions for another advantage of single-person 401(k)s.

Under the SECURE Act, effective for taxable years beginning after December 31, 2019, an employer may adopt a qualified retirement plan, including a single person 401(k) plan, up to the extended due date for the employer's federal income tax return and the plan can be retroactively effective for the taxable year. Although employee contributions can't be made after the year-end, employer contributions can be made up to the extended due date of the income tax return. See above relating to first-year owner-employee contributions for plan years beginning after December 29, 2022.

In the past, Roth 401(k) accounts had to make required minimum distributions starting on the required beginning date. (See Chapter 16.) Effective for taxable years beginning after December 31, 2023, required minimum distributions no longer apply for Roth accounts in an employer retirement plan.

The accounting for single 401(k) plans is more complicated than for IRAs, because the amounts must be tracked attributable to employer contributions, employee contributions, and taxable vs. Roth shares. Individuals with such plans are advised to get a third-party administrator to handle the accounting.

Effective for plan years beginning after December 31, 2023, an employer that doesn't sponsor another retirement plan may offer a starter 401(k) plan (or safe harbor 403(b) plan). All employees would be default enrolled in the plan at a 3% to 15% of compensation rate. Contributions would have the same limits as the regular and catch-up contributions for IRAs. (See Chapter 3.) The tax benefits of single-person 401(k) plans are better than these plans, so I don't encourage them.

---

6 Notice 2024-2

Simplified Employee Pensions (SEPs)

A Simplified Employee Pension, or SEP, is a plan alternative for self-employed persons with very low administration costs. The trade-offs are the plans are very inflexible and contributions to employee accounts are fully vested.

The employer just adopts a model plan agreement (such as Form 5305-SEP), sets up separate IRA accounts for the employees and makes contributions to the accounts by the extended due date of his or her income tax return. For most individuals, that is up to October 15 of the year following the end of the plan year. For example, if an individual return extension is filed for 2024, the contribution must be deposited by October 15, 2025.

SEPs can also be set up for small businesses other than sole proprietorships, such as corporations, S corporations, partnerships, LLCs and LLPs. These entities can have fiscal years for which the due dates of retirement plan contributions can be different from individuals.

A SEP can be adopted and funded after the year end. Under the SECURE Act, effective after 2019, so can other qualified retirement plans.

An employer can't have a SEP if it has or had any other kind of qualified retirement plan.

All eligible employees must be covered by a SEP. An eligible employee (1) has reached age 21; (2) has worked for the employer three of the last five years; and (3) has received at least $750 in compensation for 2024.

Employers can't make a SEP contribution if they have leased employees.

Employers can't discriminate in favor of highly-compensated employees, but employees covered by a collective bargaining agreement and non-resident aliens who don't have U.S. source compensation can be excluded from participating in the plan.

The maximum contribution to a SEP for 2024 is 25% of compensation for up to $345,000 of compensation, to a maximum of $69,000 for 2024 and 25% of compensation up to $350,000, to a maximum of $70,000 for 2025. Since the compensation on which the contribution is made is net of the contribution, it's effectively 20% for a self-employed person. For example, the maximum 2025 contribution for $350,000 of compensation is $350,000 - $70,000 contribution = $280,000 net compensation X 25% = $70,000. $70,000 / $350,000 = 20%. Any limit that isn't used can be carried over to succeeding years (but the contribution for 2025 still can't exceed the $70,000 limit).

Social Security can be taken into account (Social Security integration) when computing the SEP contribution.

Effective for taxable years beginning after December 31, 2022, participants have the ability to treat employer SEP contributions as Roth, in whole or in part. The employer will deposit the contributions to a designated Roth-SEP account for each employee. The Roth contributions are included in the employee's compensation. The plan must be amended before designated Roth contributions can be made.

Effective for taxable years beginning after December 29, 2022, employers of domestic employees (such as a nanny or a landscape maintenance person) may set up and make SEP contributions for them. (The SEP contributions are nondeductible for the employer.)

The employer's retirement plan reports any employer Roth contributions on behalf of an employee as a taxable distribution on Form 1099R. The amount is reported as income for the employee for the year the employer pays the contribution, not the year that the contribution relates to, so it may result in a one-year tax deferral of the taxable amount. The employer takes the tax deduction for the taxable year the contribution relates to, so there is a mismatch for the tax years of income and deduction for the employer and the employee. The employee's taxable income relating to the employer contribution isn't subject to income tax withholding or other payroll taxes, since it isn't paid to the employee. The employee should adjust his or her withholding or make estimated tax payments to avoid penalties for underpayment of estimated tax.[7]

Summary comparison Single-Person 401(k) v. SEP

Favoring the single-person 401(k):

- 100% of compensation contribution limit means a bigger contribution can be made based on less income.
- Positioning for regular 401(k) when other employees are hired.
- With a 401(k), employees can fund part of their own retirement, reducing the cost for the employer.
- 401(k) isn't subject to the tax on unrelated business taxable income for leveraged real estate.
- Employees can borrow from their 401(k) accounts. The loans are limited to the lesser of $50,000 or 50% of the present value of the participant's nonforfeitable accrued benefit. The loans must be repaid within 5 years, and the loan must be amortized on a level basis, with payments at least quarterly. Under the CARES Act, the loan limit was doubled for plan loans made by an individual during the 180-day period beginning March 27, 2020 (up to September 23, 2020) when the taxpayer was suffering COVID-19-related hardships. Required payments on outstanding loan plans that were due from March 28 through December 31, 2020 were extended for one year. The five-year loan term is also adjusted for this period. California has conformed to these relief measures. (Personally, I don't recommend these loans. They have a way of blowing up on you. Unpaid loans result in taxable income and penalties.)
- 401(k) plans can hold life insurance on the employee's life. If the life insurance proceeds are payable to the employee's estate or beneficiary or the plan trustee is required to pay the proceeds to the employee's estate or beneficiary, the employee must report taxable income for each year of coverage.

Favoring the SEP:

- No requirement to file a Form 5500 provided the alternative method of compliance requirements at Code of Federal Regulations § 2520.104-49 are met. (One-participant 401(k) plans with more than $250,000 of assets file Form 5500-EZ.)
- Can cover employees without adding expensive testing and compliance

7 Notice 2024-2

requirements at the possible cost of paying more to provide benefits for employees.
- Generally, the compliance, fees and expenses are lower for SEPs than for single-person 401(k)s.

Other retirement plan alternatives

When a business has several employees, the owner should consider other retirement plan alternatives. Some alternatives include defined benefit pension plans (payout defined based on compensation history), 401(k) plans, profit sharing plans, ESOPs, and more. SECURE 2.0 has added more Roth alternatives for these plans, except for defined benefit pension plans. A customized plan using these alternatives can help control costs of the plan and maximize the benefits to the business owner. The details are beyond the scope of this book. Consult with a retirement plan specialist to customize the optimum plan for your company.

There are many more compliance requirements for these plans, so they are much more expensive to administer and have more fiduciary duties attached to them. Annual financial audits might even be required. You should definitely get help from a pension specialist to design, establish and administer such a plan.

5

What kinds of investments can you make with a Roth or IRA?

There is a broad assortment of investments that can be held in a Roth or regular IRA account.

It's easier to say what can't be held than what can be held.

You can't hold collectibles or life insurance contracts in a Roth or IRA. Collectibles include works of art, rugs, antiques, metal, gems, stamps, coins, alcoholic beverages and other items specified by the IRS.

The IRS has announced that certain non-fungible tokens, or NFTs, might be classified as collectibles and not eligible to be held by Roths or IRAs. The purchase of a disqualified NFT by a Roth or IRA is treated as a distribution. Until the IRS issues more clear guidance, avoid investing in NFTs with your Roth or IRA.[8]

Roths and IRAs may invest in US-minted gold and silver coins and coins issued under the laws of any state. IRAs may also invest in certain platinum coins and any gold, silver, platinum, or palladium bullion of a specified fineness. *The coins must be purchased and held by the IRA custodian, not by the account owner.* Note that, while the foregoing investments may be purchased by an IRA, only cash can be contributed to an IRA, except in the case of a rollover. Note that Bitcoin cannot be contributed to an IRA, since it is not cash. There does not appear to be any prohibition against investment of IRA funds in Bitcoin.

Roths and IRAs aren't permitted to be shareholders of S corporations, except for bank stock held on October 22, 2004, so S corporation stock generally is not a permitted investment for a Roth or IRA. (Roths and IRAs can invest in limited liability companies (LLCs), which are generally taxed as passthrough entities like S corporations.)

Although banks and brokerage companies may offer what they call "self-directed" accounts, the choices might actually be limited. There are specialized companies that permit the owner of the Roth or IRA to make a broader assortment of investments. Those companies generally charge higher fees for the service, but they do not charge commissions nor are they paid by the asset sponsors. The commissions and "load" amounts paid to brokerage companies reduces the investment yield for investments held by those companies.

In addition to the prohibited investment rules, certain transactions, such as buying and selling with related parties, are also prohibited. See Chapter 7.

Note the IRS has applied a "look through" principle to Roths and IRAs to disallow personal losses on sales of securities under the "wash sale" rules when substantially identical stock and securities are purchased in a Roth or IRA account owned by the taxpayer during the period from thirty days before to thirty days after the loss sale that would otherwise

8 Notice 2023-27.

be deductible on an individual income tax return. The taxpayer's basis in the Roth or IRA account isn't adjusted for the disallowed loss. A similar theory could be applied to other transactions that haven't been specified yet.

The Roth or IRA could be required to pay income taxes on income deemed "unrelated business income," including rental income from debt-financed real estate. See Chapter 10.

Since many individuals have most of their investable assets in their retirement accounts, they should consider whether to make alternative investments with those funds. The key issues are 1) Will you have a higher return on investment on an after-tax basis compared to other alternatives?; and 2) Is the risk for this investment worth taking for the potential return? Also, be careful of asset concentration. Any investment should be part of a diversified portfolio. (Again, "unrelated business income" generated by an alternative investment may subject a Roth or IRA to unrelated business income tax. See Chapter 10.)

Growing a Roth or IRA account with an interest-charge DISC

The Sixth Circuit Court of Appeals reversed the Tax Court and allowed taxpayers to use an interest-charge domestic international sales corporation (IC-DISC) to grow Roth IRA accounts. An IC-DISC is a tax benefit allowed under the Internal Revenue Code. A U.S. export company pays a statutorily-defined "commission" to the IC-DISC. The IC-DISC can accumulate up to $10 million of untaxed income. The shareholders of the IC-DISC pay an interest charge for deferred income taxes. When the IC-DISC pays accumulated earnings out to the shareholders, they are taxable as dividends. For tax-exempt entities, including IRAs and Roth IRAs, the dividends and any gain on the disposition of DISC shares are taxed as unrelated business taxable income. (See Chapter 10.)

Summa Holdings, Inc. paid commissions to JC Export, an IC-DISC. JC Export distributed the money as a dividend to JC Holding, Inc., its sole shareholder. JC Holding, Inc. paid a 33% corporate income tax on the distribution, and then distributed the balance to its two shareholders, which were Roth IRA accounts.

The Tax Court initially upheld the IRS in disallowing the arrangement, taxing the commissions to the owners of the Roth IRA accounts. This also resulted in disallowing the deduction for the commissions for Summa Holdings, Inc. The IRS claimed in a "substance over form" argument that the arrangement allowed the Roth IRA owners to bypass the limitations on annual contributions to Roth accounts. The eventual distributions from the Roth accounts would be tax-free.

The Sixth Circuit Court of Appeals said the arrangement met the requirements under the Internal Revenue Code, and should be allowed. IC-DISCs are a creation of Congress. The Internal Revenue Code provides substance to the form of this arrangement.[9] The Ninth Circuit Court of Appeals also upheld a similar arrangement using the non-expired provisions for Foreign Sales Corporations.

The Tax Court later demonstrated that it doesn't agree with the Sixth Circuit Court of Appeals. It disallowed a similar arrangement using a Foreign Sales Corporation, another tax incentive arrangement of Congress that has been discontinued. In that case, the Tax Court

9 *Summa Holdings, Inc. v. Commissioner*, 119 AFTR 2d 2017-787, February 16, 2017

noted that the taxpayer didn't reside in the Sixth Circuit.[10] The Ninth Circuit Court of Appeals reversed the Tax Court's decision.[11]

The IC-DISC strategy might work, but be prepared for a legal fight with IRS if you don't reside in the Sixth or Ninth Circuits. The strategy is appropriate with taxpayers involved in export sales.

Note the IRS requires special disclosure for arrangements they deem to bypass the annual Roth IRA contributions limits as "listed transactions."[12] Transactions between entities owned by the Roth IRA and the owner are included in this disclosure requirement.

See Chapter 16 about Qualified Annuity Contracts, an investment alternative designed to help retirees further postpone their retirement payments from IRAs and Roths.

See Chapter 17 about valuation and retirement accounts. The IRS is paying more attention to this issue, which will increase the costs relating to having alternative investments in Roth and IRA accounts.

10 *Mazzei v. Commissioner,* 150 TC No. 7, March 5, 2018

11 *Mazzei v. Commisioner,* 127 AFTR 2d 2021-2235, 2021

12 Revenue Procedure 2004-8

6

Look before you leap! Due diligence

Since you are dealing with your retirement nest egg and accounts that represent one of the largest shares of your net worth, realize that retirement account funds should be handled with special care.

Individuals with large retirement accounts are naturally targeted by investment advisors as prospective clients. Some of them have your best interests in mind; some do not. This has more to do with character than with licensing.

Con men and women see seniors with large retirement accounts as easy prey – sheep to be shorn! You don't want to become a statistic.

The high volatility of the stock market has driven away many investors. Many are seeking alternative investments. The self-directed IRA and Roth have provided flexibility to make alternative investments. They can provide a ready source of cash for alternative investments marketed by investment brokers and advisors. Since many of these alternative investments are subject to reduced SEC disclosure and reporting regulations, it just makes it easier for the public to be more vulnerable to making investments that may not be any better than the stock market. In this way, self-directed retirement accounts can provide the mechanism to commit what may turn out be financial suicide.

What can you do to protect yourself? Either you or someone you hire should investigate the legitimacy of the investments that you are making and the individuals who are operating them. This investigation is called "due diligence."

Here are some suggested due diligence steps:

If you are investing in a business that isn't publicly traded there is significant risk of business failure. The only way to reduce this risk is to own hundreds of them, for example, in a publicly-traded mutual fund that invests in these companies.

A simple and prudent due diligence step when you are buying a piece of property is to visit it. For real estate, consider hiring an attorney to advise and assist on issues such as clear title and environmental issues.

In all cases, ask a lot of questions.

Be aware there are many operational risks when making direct investments that can result in penalties or disqualifying your account, resulting in making it immediately taxable. (See Chapter 7.) When cash is required, the amounts that can be directly invested are limited by the rules for retirement plan contributions. I suggest that you have a sanity-check meeting with an advisor familiar with these rules, who will probably talk you out of making a direct investment in an operating business or property.

Put yourself in the role of actually running the business you are considering investing in, whether it is real estate management or executing a business plan. Then ask the obvious, which are usually the scariest, questions. Does this opportunity pass the "smell test"? Are you being sold the equivalent of the Brooklyn Bridge or a company where you will make a fortune selling ice boxes to Eskimos? If your intuition tells you this "opportunity" is "too good to be true," pay attention!

Study any prospectus or financial statements that are available. If you don't understand them, bring them to a CPA or financial analyst and ask for them to explain them. If the financial statements aren't audited, understand they haven't been independently verified.

Consider hiring a CPA firm to perform a pre-acquisition study to determine if the company appears to be legitimate and look for any "skeletons in the closet." From a legal perspective, are there any unrecorded liabilities, including lease obligations, lawsuits, or warranty claims?

There are services that do background checks of people and companies. The fees are modest for online research. Also consider hiring a private investigator for a background check, including interviewing neighbors and business associates and getting credit history. If the person offering the opportunity is legitimate, he or she should readily consent to such a check and provide information to do so.

Check for current business registration with the Secretary of State. Have a title search done for real estate. Check the county recorder's office for recorded liens secured by real estate. Check Uniform Commercial Code (UCC) filings with the Secretary of State for other recorded liabilities.

If you are loaning money or buying a note, is the borrower credit worthy? Get a credit report. What is the security for the loan? Is it sufficient? Should you get an appraisal for the property securing the note? Have a lawyer prepare or review the note and security agreement.

Ask for help from a trusted lawyer, CPA or certified financial planner. Better yet, build a team of advisors to help you perform a sanity check.

Lori Greymont, President of SJREI (San Jose Real Estate Investing Association) and TV Host of the show, Funding Faceoff, shared this about due diligence on properties. She mentors real estate investors, helps them find prospective investment properties and offers passive investing opportunities. The web site for SJREI is www.sjrei.org and www.FundingFaceoff.com for the show.

> I am often asked what type of "Due Diligence" a person should do before they buy an investment property. My standard response is "that depends." While it might seem that there should be a standard checklist, there are various elements that affect how much and what type of research on a property you should perform. I have bought houses for $1,000 and others for $3,000,000…I have bought commercial property and raw land. Each type of investment comes with different types of risk, which creates a different set of due diligence investigations.

When buying a $1,000 property, you might only spend 5 minutes to review the addresses to do a little research— checking things like back taxes, water and sewer liens and any costs that would transfer to you as the buyer of the property. On a property that costs $3,000,000 we might take as much as 3 weeks, and on commercial property, we might take as much as 6 months to do the research to make sure we know what we are buying. (Editor's note – Are there any hazardous waste issues?)

Here's a list of factors that affect how much research on a property you want to complete:

1. How much is the property? Obviously if you are paying $1,000,000 you will want to do more extensive research than if you are paying $5,000.
2. What is the exit plan for the property? If you are going to sell with seller financing, you may not need to do as extensive research as you would if you were going to hold the property for a long period of time.
3. Are you buying it through a traditional method with Title Insurance and a Warranty Deed or through a Quit Claim Deed with all defects? If you are buying it through the traditional method, almost all of the liens will be discovered and cleared for you. I say "almost" because some utility or compliance liens are not always discovered, so I recommend doing the preliminary work on these as described below. If you are buying the investment with all defects, you will need to be more proactive in your investigation to make sure you know what you are buying.

Evaluate Each Property

The very first step to Due Diligence is to research the market you are investing in. I am not going to spend much time on this here, but your market will affect the performance of your investment and should not be bypassed as unimportant.

Begin by determining a geographical area in which to concentrate. It will be easier to manage your properties in the long run and will help focus your purchasing efforts. Look for neighborhoods that are stable. Use online sources for research as well as conferring with other investors.

Have a team on the ground in that area to visit the property before you buy so that you can shorten your Due Diligence time period. You can start building a ground team by calling real estate agents in the area. Interview them for an understanding of the neighborhoods you deal in. Ask for names of handymen they know—you'll need these later and those handymen may become your ground team doing your initial property drive-by assessment. When you are ready to sell, if you need the help of a professional to sell the home, make sure you go back to the people that helped you. Remember that real estate agents only get paid when they sell a house.

Data to Collect for Each Property (and where to find it!)

- MLS.com status: listed price/not listed
- Number of bedrooms, number of bathrooms, square feet
- Type of property (single family home, condo, mobile home)
- www.trulia.com listed price, neighborhood range, number of sales
- Zillow.com listed price
- Date last sold and last sold price
- County assessed value
- Parcel number
- Realestate.yahoo.com price
- FinestExpert.com price
- FinestExpert.com average rent in the area
- Property insurance
- Taxes due (call city + county tax collector)
- Water, sewer, garbage, liens, etc. (Do they stay with the house?)

A Warning About Taxes and Liens

While evaluating your property, invest time on the phone calling municipal agencies to uncover back taxes and liens. Don't rely on online data only. The information on the internet is a start, but is notoriously inaccurate. You must CALL the correct municipal offices. Realize there is a time difference, and that many offices are currently closed on Fridays. Staff is overworked and short tempered. There are long hold times. Be patient, persistent, and be prepared with your parcel number. Beware that if back taxes or liens show nothing owed, that may be because the liens were sold. Ask specific questions like, "If this was left unpaid, would it be sold at some point to someone else?" For example, in some areas of Pennsylvania, the water bill is sold like a tax lien. The bill stays with the house and can incur tens of thousands of dollars of accumulated penalties and interest in a short period of time. Plan on calling both the City and the County as they have different jurisdictions. In addition to the utility bills that stay with the property, you should investigate what compliance liens might exist on the property. These liens might occur when the lawn gets mowed by the city or your yard became the neighborhood dumping ground.

Simple Script

You'll have more luck coming across as a gentle concerned homeowner than as an investor. Government employees dislike investors, so be nice. Don't give the rest of us a bad name.

"Hi. This is Jenny Jones. I am in contract to buy a house in (city) and I'd like to find out about the current and back (taxes, bills, etc). My address is ________________ (be prepared to provide a parcel or APN number). (Get the info) Thank you. Are there any other city or county offices that I should check with? I really want to make sure I have the entire picture about this property."

Tax and Lien Checklist

- Parcel Number from county assessor
- Amount of County Taxes Owed
- City Taxes Owed
- What Utility Bills stay with the property?
    - Water, Sewer, Garbage, Electric, Gas
- Are any of these owed?
- Existing Code Violations or Fines
- Have tax liens been sold?
- Is the property on a list for a tax sale?

Property Insurance

As you navigate the property process, it's crucial to include insurance considerations in your due diligence checklist, especially in states like California and Florida, where insurance costs can be significantly impacted by natural disasters such as wildfires and hurricanes. In California, many insurance companies are not writing new policies due to the increasing frequency and severity of wildfires, which have led to substantial losses. This situation has created a challenging market where obtaining coverage can be difficult and costly. Rising premiums and limited availability can affect your overall budget and financial planning. By proactively researching insurance options, understanding potential costs, and assessing the specific risks associated with your desired property, you can make a more informed decision and avoid unexpected expenses down the line.

Property Inspection

After you have determined what is owed, the next part of Due Diligence is to understand the condition of the property. It is best to start out with a general property inspection. Not all states require that property inspectors be licensed or certified, so the quality of the inspection may vary. Also, many property inspectors make their money on the repairs that they identify. It is best to locate a licensed (certified) property inspector who has no ulterior motive for the inspection except to educate you on the property condition.

Other types of inspections that you may want to order in addition to a general inspection may include roof, heating and cooling, foundation, and structural and pest inspections. If you are buying in an area that is known for termite infestations, then I would add the pest inspections to the "must" have list of inspections together with the property inspection.

Again, all of this comes back to the purpose and cost of the property. Let's say you may be buying a $5,000 property that you plan to sell to another buyer with financing in place. If this is the case, you may only want a property inspection and termite inspection.

On the other hand, let's say you are buying a $500,000 house that you want to renovate and rent out. In that case, it would be worth the money to order the rest of the inspections to mitigate the chance of buying any costly and unforeseen future issues.

(Editor's note. Also be aware that an IRA-killing prohibited transaction results when an IRA owner provides any service, such as repairs, maintenance, or improvements. Those services should be provided by unrelated contractors. (See Chapter 7.))

Evaluate the Data

The first time you are ready to evaluate all the data you have collected, get experienced assistance. In general, you want to acquire properties where you have room in the price and additional costs to have multiple exit plans for the property should your main plan not work out. Since it is nearly impossible in this current economy to concretely state what a property is worth, you have to do your best by estimating. Talk to others who are investing and selling in the same area that you are to get a better value comparison and then make your decision.

Finally, I want to encourage you to not get stuck on trying to recover your research costs and time by forcing the deal to work. If you have done your research, you should know whether the house will work for your planned exit or not. Don't try to force it to work because you want to do a deal. Many "homeowners" buy emotionally, not logically. Unfortunately, so do many investors. Emotion justifies doing a bad deal when the numbers don't support it. The numbers will either work or they won't. If they don't, quickly move on to your next property. You may lose a little money on the due diligence research, but in the long run, you will earn more money on the profitable deals you do, than the costs on the deals you don't do. Also, the amount of time you lose on a deal that won't work can never be recovered. As an investor, if you focus on the numbers and performance of your portfolio of investments over the long run, you will be successful.

Some Additional Thoughts on Due Diligence for Real Estate

Craig Martin, Master of Science of Financial Services (MSFS), CFP® and President of The Family Wealth Consulting Group, offered these additional thoughts about due diligence for direct real estate investments. Mr. Martin also manages and co-invests with his clients into four alternative investment funds that include a combination of real estate, pre-IPO stock, early investments in start-up businesses as angel investors plus direct loans to people and businesses.

For my clients who want to invest in real estate, we start with a realization that when added to a stock and bond portfolio, direct investment in real estate is a superior risk management tool because it is not stocks or bonds. Reducing price volatility by allocating 15% or more of their investment assets into real estate, prudent investors can expect to earn higher terminal values during the growth years, as well as spending more income during their retirement years. Those two benefits can last a lifetime, by maintaining a desired allocation into real estate.

Over the last 21 years, we have been investing in real estate limited partnerships that are managed by experts who have a track record of earning higher returns than the historical 10% returns we could expect in the stock market. This is a 'hands off' investment because we only write the check which then hires the general partner, or fund manager, to buy the address, manage it to increase its value, and then sell it, with no financial liability to us as investors greater than our initial investment. This is called a Real Estate Limited Partnership (RELP), where the general partner has all the work as well as all the financial and legal responsibility, while the investor just has their original investment at risk.

I consider it a serious responsibility to maintain the highest level of fiduciary responsibility towards my clients, providing transparency, full disclosure and honesty. With that fiduciary responsibility in mind, I have performed hundreds of due diligence reports on real estate experts acting as general partners in our limited partnerships.

My research includes confirming that the general partner has more than a 10-year track record of earning an average of a 15% compounded annual return, or better. Then I make sure they have their own money in the limited partnership as well as a contract that we both share in the profits that the general partner has earned when they sell the underlying address. Both features ensure to me that the general partner is going to strive to maximize profits, and hopefully generate a return in excess of 15%, compounded annually.

Since the general partner and I each have our own money in this investment and share in the back-end profits, I am confident when they present a deal to me that they have performed the best due diligence on selecting the best address, an address with the most potential for profits based on the local demographic data including population growth, average salary, diversification of the local industry, a potential for increasing rent due to average salary versus average cost to rent or buy. It is that 'affordability to rent or buy' calculation that is a critical source of accessing the best demographics.

My wife and I co-invest with our clients, ultimately investing a minimum of 15% of our total portfolio, into an increasingly diversified portfolio of real estate each year, so that, after 5 years of investments, we now own 180 different addresses, managed by 35 general partners, across 3-5 business cycles, in 21 different states allocated among 13 different categories, such as single family, multi-family apartments, commercial, senior living, etc.

We have registered a service mark for the phrase, "Diversification Is Your Only Safety"®, and, as you can see, we focus our investment recommendations by that statement.

Based on our experience we expect that private equity, including real estate, can earn returns greater than we normally expect from the efficient public stock market, because of the inefficiency of the private markets.

That inefficiency is demonstrated when managers of a limited partnership have a history of buying real estate at discounts of sometimes 25%, or more to fair market values. A classic description of how this consistently happens is when a small apartment complex is owned by an inexperienced couple, who typically don't maintain the property up to par and spend all the net cash flow received from rents. Because of inadequate maintenance during many years of ownership, the value of the property depreciates compared to the local market prices. Because of inexperience and mismanagement, rental rates and occupancy typically drop compared to the local competition. The sales price of this property for a savvy buyer can be significantly below competitive market prices. Experienced real estate general partners, such as our chosen fund managers, are prepared to buy such a property on quick notice, providing what the seller wants most, which is immediate cash plus a guarantee of closing escrow quickly.

Clearly, it is the nature of experienced and quality managers of real estate limited partnerships to regularly buy, add value, increase rents and then liquidate while earning returns of mid-teens or higher, in an expected 5-year hold period. It is true that all RELP's are self-liquidating. That means, for savvy investors, if you want some fixed allocation of 15% or greater to real estate as a percentage of your total portfolio, then you must reinvest principal from sales to maintain your chosen allocation. The profits are taxable in a long term capital gains tax bracket with a choice to be reinvested or spent.

When new clients ask me to analyze their own privately owned real estate investments, finding earned or projected returns in mid-teens or higher is very rare in my practice. For the most part, individual investors have very limited investment methodologies, where all they will talk about is to buy and hold *forever* plus an effort to *pay off the mortgage,* relegating their portfolio, based on my analysis, to earning expected returns that are usually under 8% compounded annually. That is less than ½ of what the professionally-managed portfolios that we offer have been earning for our clients.

Alternatively, you can hire a certified financial planner (CFP) who is also a Registered Investment Adviser (RIA). The RIA is compensated by fees, never by commissions. An RIA, trained as a CFP, has a fiduciary responsibility to their clients, in contrast to a broker paid exclusively by commissions who works for a large brokerage company (think UBS, Merrill Lynch, Bank of America, etc.). There are very few RIA's with a CFP who also manage real estate in their client's portfolios. You can find such an RIA as members of an industry organization called ADISA.

7

What kinds of transactions must you avoid with your Roth or IRA? (Prohibited transactions.)

When you have a self-directed Roth or IRA account, it can feel like you have a tax-sheltered checkbook. As I discussed in Chapter 5, there is a wide range of choices of possible investments that you can make using these accounts.

The liberalized ability to convert other accounts to Roth accounts is especially exciting, because by meeting fairly liberal requirements, amounts withdrawn from a Roth are tax-free. (Of course, there is that small problem of paying the income taxes for a conversion…) Not only that, but you aren't required to take required minimum distributions during your lifetime. A former advantage of Roth accounts, the ability to continue contributing to the account when you have personal service income and you are older than age 70 ½ (or the applicable age for required minimum distributions), was extended to regular IRAs by the SECURE Act of 2019, effective for tax years beginning after December 31, 2019.

In order to have the most choices of investments, you will probably have to use a custodian that is not a traditional bank, brokerage company or mutual fund. Conventional custodians will offer a more restricted menu of choices.

There are three constraints to be concerned about:

1. Roths and IRAs aren't permitted to own some investments, like collectibles and S corporation stock. See Chapter 5.

2. Roths and IRAs can be subject to income taxes on Unrelated Business Taxable Income when debt is used to finance the investment or the investment is deemed to be a trade or business operation. This is not a deal killer, but should be considered when estimating your return on investment for an investment alternative. (Note employer retirement plans, like 401(k) plans, aren't subject to this requirement. Most of them won't offer alternative investments. See Chapter 4 for details about single-person 401(k) plans.) See Chapter 10 for details about the Unrelated Business Income Tax.

3. Certain transactions aren't permitted for Roths and IRAs. They are called "prohibited transactions," and can result in disqualification of the account and immediate taxation.

In this chapter, I'm going to focus on prohibited transactions. I am only going to hit some highlights so you will be aware of some red flags. When you are using a self-directed Roth or IRA for alternative investments (investments other than stocks, bonds, savings accounts and mutual funds), you should consult with a team of advisors including an investment advisor, a tax advisor (CPA, enrolled agent, enrolled actuary or tax attorney) and an attorney schooled in retirement accounts. Some self-directed custodians have a directory of professionals familiar with the rules to help you.

As part of its service, a custodian for a self-directed Roth or IRA account should educate its clients about prohibited transactions and watch the activity of its account owners for potential prohibited transactions.

Prohibited transactions are defined primarily at Internal Revenue Code Section 4975.

For IRAs and Roth IRAs, ***the penalty for a prohibited transaction is disqualification of the account and acceleration of any taxable income.***[13] The account is considered to be distributed on the first day of the year during which the prohibited transaction happened. An extreme penalty such as this dictates that the IRA owner must give serious attention to avoiding prohibited transactions. If there are any investments that are sensitive and could result in a prohibited transaction, they should be held in separate IRA or Roth IRA accounts to insulate other retirement assets from exposure to the disqualification penalty.

For many purposes, such as computing required minimum distributions, a taxpayer's IRA accounts are combined and treated as one account. (See Chapter 16.) Effective for taxable years beginning after December 29, 2022, SECURE Act 2.0 clarifies that when disqualifying an IRA account for a prohibited transaction, each IRA account is treated separately. Nothing in the new provision is to be construed as inferring the proper treatment of individual retirement accounts as one plan in the case of any other provisions of the Internal Revenue Code. (I haven't seen a case of the accounts being combined for a disqualification before.)

The penalty for other (employer) retirement accounts is a 15% excise tax on the amount involved. If the prohibited transaction isn't timely corrected, an excise tax of 100% of the amount involved can be imposed. The excise tax is reported on Form 5330. You can find the form at www.irs.gov.

Red flags should go up any time there is a transaction between the Roth or IRA and a "party in interest" (also called "disqualified persons"). A party in interest includes a plan fiduciary (custodian or owner), and family members of the account owner including the spouse, descendants (children, grandchildren) and their spouses, and ancestors (parents, grandparents) and their spouses, and entities controlled (50% or more of capital interest or voting power) by a fiduciary or listed family member of the owner or fiduciary. Employees and 10% owners of capital or profits of controlled entities are also parties in interest. However, employees aren't disqualified persons unless they are highly compensated, meaning they individually earn 10% or more of the aggregate wages paid by the employer.

I'm not going to discuss this in depth, but here are a few items to be aware of:

- The owner of the account can't use or rent a house owned by the account. However, a house can be rented at fair market value to an unrelated person or to a brother or sister of the owner. In the case of renting to a brother or sister, be sure the rent is at fair market rates or you could violate party-in-interest rules or the "exclusive benefit rule."

- The owner of the account may not handle cash (currency) for the entity or pay

---

13 Internal Revenue Code § 408(e)(2)

expenses for the entity from a petty cash fund or for reimbursement by the entity.

- To avoid accidentally tripping yourself, it's probably best to hire an independent property manager to collect rents and pay expenses of real estate investments.

- The owner can't "do the work" to rehabilitate an investment property. (No tearing out sheet rock and hammering new sheet rock yourself!) The owner should find an unrelated independent contractor to do the work.

- The Roth or IRA can't make a loan to the owner or a disqualified person, but can make a loan to a brother or sister of the owner, or to any unrelated person or an indirect relative, like an uncle or an aunt. The loan should be handled in a businesslike manner, with a written note and security, and paid promptly. The transaction should not be a disguised gift. Again, when renting to a relative such as a brother or sister, the rent should be at a market rate.

- A Roth or IRA can participate in an investment together with a disqualified person, such as forming a new C corporation (not S corporation) or limited liability company (LLC). The rationale for this position is there is no prohibited transaction for setting up the arrangement at inception because the disqualified interest doesn't exist until the entity is formed.[14] You need to be very careful in operating these entities to avoid prohibited transactions after the entity is formed. The entity must be adequately funded to avoid having to make additional capital contributions in the future. It can also be sticky if one of the investors decides to stop participating and has to be bought out!

  As an example of an operational disqualification, an IRA was disqualified because the IRA owner, when the IRA owned the majority of an LLC, received wages as general manager of the LLC. The IRA owner received wages of $9,754 in 2005 and $29,263 in 2006. His taxable income from termination of the IRA exceeded $300,000 plus penalties and interest. Don't plan on acquiring a business using your Roth or IRA and drawing a salary from it.[15]

- Capital contributions can be made by an IRA to an entity wholly owned by the IRA, such as a single member LLC, without a prohibited transaction problem, due to an exemption for an intra-company transfer.

- Capital contributions can also be made to an entity provided the disqualified person doesn't own 50% or more of the entity (including the ownership interests of any other direct relatives, collectively).[16] We are talking about a very delicate subject here. Only proceed with professional guidance.

- The Roth or IRA can't buy real estate from a disqualified person.

When the account owner meets requirements, such as reaching age 59 1/2, he or she can distribute assets, such as a house, from a Roth account tax-free. So, a strategy to buy

14 *Swanson v. Commissioner*, 106 T.C. No. 76, February 14, 1996

15 *Ellis*, 2015-1 U.S.T.C. ¶ 50,328, June 5, 2015

16 Internal Revenue Code § 4975(e)(2)(G)

a retirement home could be to buy it in a Roth account, rent it to someone other than a disqualified person until it's paid off (subject to unrelated business income tax on the financed part of income), and then distribute it tax-free after retirement.

Possible "cure" for a prohibited transaction

If you make a "foot fault" and have a prohibited transaction, all may not be lost. You can apply to the Department of Labor for an exemption from the prohibited transaction rules. The exemption can be retroactive. This is an expensive and time-consuming process but can be worth it to avoid disqualification of your account.

The Department of Labor has published a procedure to apply for an exemption, RIN 1210-AB49, 2011 ARD 207-1 (October 27, 2011) and regulations (ESBA final regulations, 76 FR 66637, October 27, 2011) explaining the procedure to apply for an exemption. A web page with details is https://www.dol.gov/agencies/ebsa/laws-and-regulations/rules-and-regulations/exemptions/class/pte-procedures#:~:text=The%20Secretary%20of%20Labor%20is%20authorized%20to%20grant,an%20exemption%20procedure%20to%20provide%20for%20such%20exemptions. Get professional help with preparing this application.

Expansion of Employee Plans Compliance Resolution System

SECURE 2.0 makes traditional IRAs and Roth IRAs eligible for the Employee Plans Compliance Resolution System (EPCRS) under Revenue Procedure 2021-20. This system is intended for taxpayers to correct minor failures in the plan document or in the operation of the plan. Congress specified the penalty for failures to make required minimum distributions and disallowed rollovers from inherited IRAs by a nonspouse beneficiary. (See Chapters 16 and 19.) The IRS is directed to issue guidance about the procedures, some of which can be done with automatic IRS consent, within two years after December 29, 2022. The IRS issued interim guidance in Notice 2023-43. The majority of the operational failures for employer retirement plans relate to plan loans, which are prohibited for a party in interest for traditional and Roth IRAs. It would be great if some prohibited transaction "foot faults" were resolved without disqualifying the account under this system.

8

Making alternative investments in a Roth or IRA using a self-directed account

Many securities brokerage companies and banks offer "self-directed" IRA and Roth accounts. Although these plans do offer some flexibility, they typically offer a menu of choices that doesn't include alternatives like private mortgages, real estate, and non-publicly traded business investments.

Companies have been created that offer custodian services permitting holding these alternative investments.

There is a price to be paid to have this flexibility in the form of higher fees and potentially higher risk.

Also see Chapter 17 about annual valuation requirements for alternative investments.

When choosing one of these custodians, do some investigation or due diligence. (See Chapter 6 for some approaches.) Is the company substantial so that you can rely on it to continue in existence to hold your assets? What safeguards or oversight is it subject to? Is it regulated? Does it have audited financial statements? Does the company provide education or other information about your responsibilities in maintaining a self-directed account? Does the company monitor potential prohibited transactions that could subject the account owner to a penalty or plan disqualification? Is it a member of the Retirement Industry Trust Association (RITA), the association for such regulated custodians?

Some alternative investments can result in taxable income for a Roth or IRA. See Chapter 10, "When IRAs and Roths pay taxes." In most cases, the account owner is responsible for having the tax returns prepared for the IRA or Roth. Since the unrelated business income tax is one of the most complex areas of the Internal Revenue Code, you should probably hire a professional tax return preparer who is familiar with the rules to prepare the income tax returns. This is an additional expense to consider when deciding to use a self-directed IRA and to make an investment subject to the tax versus other alternatives.

The checkbook LLC

Having another operating entity owned by the Roth or IRA can provide three important advantages:

1 Institutions tend to move slowly. You could identify an opportunity, such as buying a foreclosed property on the courthouse steps, but not have access to

the cash in time to take advantage of it. If the cash is held in an operating entity, a cashier's check can be immediately generated.

2 Many custodians charge fees for each transaction. If you are paying bills for operating a business or a rental property, you could write hundreds of checks in a year. You can avoid per transaction fees by paying the bills using a checking account for an operating entity.

3 Some investments can involve risks that could impact other assets owned by the Roth or IRA. You can isolate those risks, protecting other assets owned by the Roth or IRA, using a limited liability "envelope," like a corporation or limited liability company. (In addition, you can and probably should set up a separate IRA or Roth account to hold the investment that you wish to isolate.)

Making the decision to form an entity involves important legal issues, so I recommend that you consult with an attorney before going ahead. I also recommend that you use an attorney to form the entity and to monitor its operations to assure you qualify for the liability protection that you are trying to accomplish.

In most cases, the best entity form for the operating entity is a Limited Liability Company (LLC). LLCs can have a manager (the account owner) that is different from the owner (the IRA or Roth). Single-owner LLCs are generally "disregarded entities" for income tax reporting. That means any taxable activities are reported on the income tax return for the IRA or Roth, and any transaction of the single-member LLC is deemed to be a transaction of the IRA or Roth. It also means the LLC itself is generally not subject to income taxes. In contrast, a "regular" or "C" corporation must file its own income tax returns and pay income taxes.

Be aware an LLC can have its own tax or other compliance requirements. In California, a single-member LLC must file an annual report, Form 568. In addition, LLCs registered in California pay an annual $800 tax and those with $250,000 or more of California-source gross receipts pay an annual "fee" of $900 to $11,790 based on the amount of gross receipts. The tax and fee apply even when the LLC has an operating loss! (The California Franchise Tax Board's web site is www.ftb.ca.gov.)

California LLCs must also file a Statement of Information plus a filing fee every two years with the California Secretary of State.

Reporting requirements vary from state to state, so check the requirements for the states your LLC is organized in and the states your LLC operates in. You can do it online, but you can shortcut the process for a fee by using a tax consultant or attorney.

Note: The following explanation for the Business Ownership Information Report has been suspended by a nationwide preliminary injunction by a U.S. District Court in Texas (*Texas Top Cop Shop v. Garland*, December 3, 2024, U.S. District Court, Eastern District of Texas, Case No. 4:24-CV-478.) The federal government is expected to appeal the ruling. For updates, see www.fincen.gov/boi and your tax and legal advisors. At this time, according to the FinCEN web site, reporting is voluntary.

Most LLCs (and corporations) are required to file a Business Ownership Information Report with the Financial Crimes Information Network (FinCEN). LLCs that were created before January 1, 2024 are required to submit the report by December 31, 2024. LLCs created during 2024 are required to submit the report within 90 days after creation. LLCs created after 2024 are required to submit the report within 30 days after creation. For details, consult with your attorney or tax advisors and see www.fincen.gov/boi.

Since a single member LLC is a disregarded entity, it is subject to the same prohibited transaction restrictions as the IRA or Roth. See chapter 7 on prohibited transactions. Avoid expensive litigation with the IRS by avoiding prohibited transactions. Remember the penalty is current taxation of the account balance as of the beginning of the year of the prohibited transaction! An owner-manager should avoid loans and avoid handling currency. It's better to have a property manager collect rent and pay expenses for investment properties.

In some cases, you might want the Roth or IRA to make a joint investment with a "party in interest" or "disqualified person." These investments must be handled with special care. You should assure there is adequate funding when the investment is formed, because additional investments after formation may be prohibited transactions. See chapter 7.

(Advisors don't agree on the desirability of checkbook LLCs. For example, Tom Anderson, President of the Retirement Industry Trust Association (RITA), commented that RITA generally does not favor checkbook LLCs because they tend to be used to deliberately circumvent custodial procedure designed to prevent prohibited transactions or lead unintentionally to prohibited transactions because owners are not familiar with the ever-changing landscape. Some RITA member firms require that owners of single-member IRA-owned LLCs sign a contract agreeing to acquire the services of a qualified professional (CPA or attorney) to review all LLC transactions in advance of execution for compliance with the rules before they will allow the owner to create the LLC with their firm. This requirement enables the IRA owner to take advantage of the benefits of a single-member LLC, while providing extra protection to avoid a violation of the prohibited transaction rules. He believes they will probably be prohibited in the future if the Department of Labor continues to see prohibited transaction violations involving checkbook LLCs.)

Conclusion

The decision to make alternative investments using a self-directed account is an important one. The price is additional expense, complexity, investment risk, and exposure for potential prohibited transactions. When the account owner is operating in an area that he or she understands or with the assistance of a skilled investment advisor, CPA or attorney and can generate significantly greater returns, plus get greater investment diversification in the process, using a self-directed IRA or Roth, possibly together with a checkbook LLC, can make sense.

9
A case study

Dick Blakeley, CEO of The Blakeley Group, Inc., a registered investment advisor firm, volunteered to provide this case study/example of an actual client situation where a self-directed IRA was used to accomplish a client's financial goals. The web site for The Blakeley Group, Inc. is www.theblakeleygroup.com.

Scenario: A small manufacturing and distribution company was doing a business of several million dollars in sales. It is slightly profitable and has positive cash flow. The company had about $500,000 in accounts receivable and $500,000 in inventory. The cash flow for the company was tight because of new orders. The company could obtain volume discounts based on the size of the orders. Previously, the company had borrowed just enough funds through a factoring company to keep inventory on the shelf. To add to the challenge, one of the companies that had financed inventory had filed for Chapter 11 Bankruptcy.

Another problem the company had was that the factoring company was charging about 24% per year and was costing the company a significant amount of its pre-tax earnings. Many small banks do not lend to this type of company. The company at any one time had about $600,000 in receivables being factored and the cost was about $144,000 per month in cash flow. The company realized if it could bring down the interest it paid for factoring: a) the cash flow would more than double, and b) the company could more than triple its earnings.

The owners of the company had friends and family who had IRAs and retirement plans with big balances and who were earning less than 4% interest on the funds deposited in their plans. In addition, the owners believed those same friends and family members would be willing to invest part of their funds in a fixed income note secured with the inventory and receivables in the company if only there was a way to make such an investment.

The owners of the company had an "Aha!" moment and came up with a winning solution for both the company and their friends who had low-earning IRAs. The company owners spoke with their friends to see how many would truly like to participate in such a note and they got great feedback on the idea. They worked with their CPA and their attorney and found out there was an opportunity to create a Limited Liability Company (LLC) as a lending facility.

The LLC would be owned by IRAs and individuals and could be managed by the owners of the IRAs and the individual investors. (Note that owners of the company and some of their relatives, including their IRAs, couldn't participate to avoid a prohibited transaction. The ownership structure of the LLC should be reviewed by an attorney to assure the prohibited transaction rules aren't violated. Also, an individual who is an owner of an IRA shouldn't invest in the same LLC as their IRA.) The LLC made agreements with the company to lend capital to the company at better rates than the factoring company. In return, the LLC would receive monthly cash from the company and the LLC would be the lien holder on the receivables and the inventory. The LLC would be listed as one of the beneficiaries on a key-man life insurance policy and the company has E&O insurance to cover the principals of the company.

An LLC was formed to receive funds from IRAs and individuals to lend to the manufacturing company. In return for the loans, the LLC held a security interest in the inventory and the receivables. Contracts were made with the manufacturing company with terms to include the interest to be paid, the collateral being secured, an agreement accounting for the collateral and the aging of receivables, the rate of discount to be used to provide a margin of safety for the investors, and an agreement that the company would pay all accounting, legal, and professional fees.

The LLC managers have an independent party receive the monthly cash flow, pay taxes, prepare taxes, pay the investors, and bi-annually verify the collateral owned by the company but secured by the LLC and send out periodic letters to the note holders updating on their work and observations on the accounts receivables and inventory.

The loan documents include an important clause allowing for substitution of collateral by the company. This is important because the inventory is turning over and the accounts receivable are being paid and new accounts receivable generated. The LLC filed a Uniform Commercial Code (UCC) statement with the state and county to codify the terms of the loan between the company and the LLC and notify all other potential lenders that the terms of the loan needed to be satisfied and the collateral be released before another lender could use the collateral for another loan.

Here are some key points:

- The interest rate needs to follow state law guidelines as to the maximum interest it can collect and pay (anti-usury rules). If the rates are above the rate given in the guidelines, the LLC will need to apply for a special lending license.
- Investors like and need to be kept informed on the issues around the loans.
- The investors need to fully accept that there is and will be no liquid market for the loan and, as a result, they need to agree to the reality that they may need to hold onto the loan until the note matures.
- In this kind of a private transaction, the LLC needs its own independent counsel/attorney to represent the LLC.
- The LLC's attorney needs to prepare documentation for the investors to verify that they have the means and the sophistication to invest in the private note.
- The LLC's attorney needs to prepare and see the loan documents with the company fully executed, including the UCC filings.

End Result...

The company replaced its high-priced debt with a five year note for which it pays 10% to private investors using part of the investors' retirement funds. The private investors received significantly higher interest rates than they would have received from their banks or credit unions and the investors felt comfortable because their investment in the LLC's note was collateralized. Both sides benefited from the other's needs.

Epilogue...

The company paid interest as agreed for more than four of the loan's five-year term and the owner died in a car crash. The loan was fully repaid with the proceeds from the key man's life insurance policy and the owner's spouse sold the company to its employees.

Notes from Michael Gray –

Private loans can be good investments for self-directed IRAs, because interest income isn't subject to tax to the IRA or Roth as unrelated business taxable income. In Dick's case study, the interest rate is attractive and the note is secured with accounts receivable and inventory. You still need to be careful to avoid loans to certain related parties (including companies owned by certain family members), which can be prohibited transactions. I would prefer to have the management of the LLC be independent of the management of the company that is borrowing the funds. See Chapters 7 and 8.

10

When Roths and IRAs owe income taxes – The Unrelated Business Income Tax

Many people aren't aware that "tax exempt" entities, including charities and retirement plans, are subject to income taxes on certain types of income, called "unrelated business taxable income." How to apply the tax rules for unrelated business taxable income is one of the more complex areas of the income tax laws.

Just because an activity owned by a Roth or IRA is subject to unrelated business income tax doesn't mean you shouldn't do it. The key issues are: 1) What is the net return on investment after income taxes and compliance costs? and 2) What is the risk to get that return? If the return is greater than your other alternatives with a reasonable risk, it can be favorable to go ahead with the activity. With low interest rates paid for certificates of deposit issued by banks and a volatile stock market, many people will find it hard to keep up with inflation without making alternative investments.

The federal tax form on which the income tax is computed for tax-exempt entities is Form 990-T, Exempt Organization Income Tax Return. You can get a copy of the form and instructions at the IRS web site, www.irs.gov.

When tax-exempt trusts, like retirement accounts, are subject to the tax on unrelated business income, they are generally taxed under the rules and rates that apply to trusts. The first $1,000 of unrelated business income is not subject to tax. For 2024, taxable income over $15,200 is subject to the 37% maximum federal income tax rate. For 2025, the threshold is $15,650.

For example, when many real estate properties are bought and sold during a tax year in "quick turn" transactions, these transactions may be determined to be a trade or business. ("Occasional" sales of properties, especially without rehabilitation, is not a trade or business. The crossover point from "investor" to "dealer" hasn't been clearly defined.) The properties are not considered to be held for investment, but for sale to customers in the ordinary course of a trade or business. These transactions and related business expenses should be reported as unrelated business income.

The IRS has "looked through" an IRA to find a "wash sale" for a sale of securities by the participant and purchase by the IRA. For many purposes, the IRS treats multiple IRA accounts as one account, such as when computing required minimum distributions. This may be an indication the IRS could try to aggregate "quick sale" transactions in multiple IRA accounts to find a trade or business, resulting in unrelated business income.

Another type of activity that is probably a business is subdividing land and building homes for resale.

There is a special exception for property purchased by a tax-exempt entity from a

financial institution in conservatorship or receivership or from the conservator or receiver of such a financial institution. The property must have been identified within the 9-month period beginning on the date of its acquisition as property held for sale, but no more than one-half of property acquired in a single transaction may be designated. The sale must take place before the later of (1) the date 30 months after the date of acquisition of the property, or (2) a date otherwise specified by the IRS. While the property is held by the tax-exempt entity, the total expenditures on improvements and development activities included in the basis of the property may not exceed 20% of the net selling price of the property.

Trade or business income of a partnership or an S corporation for which the tax-exempt entity has an ownership interest is unrelated business income. There is a special exception for S corporation employer shares held by an Employee Stock Ownership Plan (ESOP). IRAs and Roths aren't permitted shareholders for S corporations anyway.

Any income received from a "controlled entity," including rental income which would usually not be subject to tax, is taxed as net unrelated trade or business income.

Generally, rental income from rental real estate is not unrelated business income, but see below about debt-financed income. Rent from personal property that is incidental to renting real estate is also not unrelated business income. To be "incidental," the rent for the personal property may not exceed 10% of the total rents for all property leased.

Gains from the sale of real estate are also generally not unrelated business income, unless the property is inventory or held for sale to customers in a trade or business, or the gain is debt-financed income.

Unrelated debt-financed income

Real estate is an especially attractive investment vehicle because you can use leverage to enhance your returns. This means you can finance a big portion of the purchase price and control a big value of property with a relatively small cash investment.

When you use leverage to purchase property in an IRA or Roth, a proportionate part of the income, including rental income and gain when the property is sold, is unrelated business taxable income. A percentage (an average of the acquisition indebtedness divided by the average adjusted basis of the property during the period it's held by the organization during the taxable year) is applied to the income and deductions to compute the amounts to be reported on the unrelated business tax return.

There is a special exception from the unrelated debt-financed income rule for company retirement accounts, such as 401(k)s (including single-person or solo 401(k)s), profit-sharing plans and pension plans (but not Simplified Employee Pensions (SEPs)) and government retirement accounts. The fact that you can make leveraged investments in real estate that are exempt from the unrelated business income tax makes company retirement accounts very attractive compared to IRAs or Roths, which are not exempt when they engage in leveraged transactions.

Since the custodian firms for self-directed IRA accounts typically don't prepare the tax forms for unrelated business income tax and the tax is complex, you should consider having the tax return for unrelated business tax prepared by a professional tax return preparation firm who is familiar with the tax.

11

Where to get help with your investments

Where can you get investment advice to guide you during turbulent times, including information about alternative investments?

A resource to consider in most communities is the fee-only Certified Financial Planner (CFP®). These individuals have received considerable education relating to investing and personal financial management. They have learned to deal with a client's total financial picture. Since their income is solely based on fees, they don't have a financial interest in the investment decisions of their clients and so can provide independent advice.

I suggest that you watch my television interviews with financial planner Craig Martin, CFP® entitled "Investing In Turbulent Times" and "The Role of the Fee-Only Financial Planner." You can find them on YouTube under my YouTube channel, financialinsiderweek (@financialinsiderweekly.) (By the way, this television series was strictly educational and a great source of financial education. I discontinued producing the show late in 2017, but many of the interviews are still relevant.)

There are also community education groups where you can get information. Such a group in Silicon Valley is the San Jose Real Estate Investing Association. You can get information about their meetings at www.sjrei.org.

Learn to distinguish gambling and speculation (short-term, high-risk trades) versus investing (long-term).

Study investment books to make more informed decisions. A classic book on securities investing is *A Random Walk Down Wall Street.* Another book to look at is Nick Murray's book, *Simple Wealth, Inevitable Wealth.*

12

Creating a bigger account – rollovers from qualified plans (401(k) accounts)

When advisors suggest considering investing in alternative investments in a Roth or IRA account, people often object, "I don't have very much available in my Roth or IRA to invest!"

The advisor may then ask, "Do you have a 401(k) or other retirement plan at work?"

"Yes, I have a 401(k) account with about $100,000 in it."

It may be that the $100,000 401(k) balance can be rolled over to a Roth or IRA account. (Of course, the rollover to a Roth could be taxable. See Chapter 13. If the 401(k) account was a Roth 401(k) account, the rollover generally wouldn't be taxable.)

New fiduciary rules make it harder for financial advisors to recommend rollovers. It's easier for them if the account owner simply requests a rollover.

Subject to plan limitations, retirement accounts are portable. With a few limitations, funds can be rolled over from employer retirement accounts to a Roth or IRA account and, in some cases, from a Roth or IRA account to an employer retirement account. We used to be concerned with segregating rollover funds from qualified plans for future rollovers to other qualified plans. This is no longer a concern. Even partial rollovers are permitted and you don't have to be more than age 59 1/2 to qualify if the distribution is made as a direct "trustee to trustee" transfer.

Not all employer plans permit such an "in service" transfer, so that can be an issue. Perhaps the employer can be persuaded to amend the plan to permit such transfers.

Any pretax (taxable) employee contributions from an employer plan are first allocated to direct "trustee to trustee" transfers. Any pretax amounts in excess of direct transfers are next allocated according to the participant's selection of plans that receive 60-day rollovers. Any remaining pretax amounts are allocated to cash received and are taxable income. In order to qualify for this treatment, the recipient plan must agree to separately account for after-tax contributions.[17]

When making the above allocations, the pretax amounts are computed using a ratio of the pretax contributions to the total value of the account before the distribution. For example, Jane Employee elects to distribute $100,000 from a 401(k) account with a $250,000 balance and to which Jane made $50,000 of nondeductible contributions. The pretax portion of the distribution is $200,000 / $250,000 = 80% X $100,000 = $80,000.

If Jane received the $100,000 distribution in cash and elected to rollover $80,000 to a regular IRA and $20,000 to a Roth account within 60 days of receiving the distribution, Jane

17 Notice 2014-54, September 18, 2014, REG-105739-11, September 18, 2014

can designate the after-tax amount would be allocated to the $20,000 rollover amount to the Roth account, so there would be no taxable income from the Roth conversion, and allocation of the $80,000 pretax to the regular IRA for continued tax deferral.

Work with the employer and Roth or IRA custodian to timely complete any paperwork required to designate where the pretax amount is being allocated and request direct rollovers.

Required minimum distributions and hardship distributions can't be rolled over from an employer plan to a Roth or IRA. Those must be taken first.

Distributions from an employer retirement account of amounts that would otherwise be taxable are subject to 20% federal income tax withholding, which can make completing a rollover of the entire amount difficult. You can avoid income tax withholding by making a direct "trustee to trustee" transfer, instead of a cash distribution followed by a rollover.

Advantages of having the funds in a Roth IRA or regular IRA account include to possibly have a better selection of investments and the ability to make alternative investments for more diversification, such as investing in pre-IPO stock, real estate, and private money mortgages. (See Chapter 5.)

The disadvantage of having the funds in a Roth or IRA account is the assets might have less bankruptcy protection, particularly if the funds were contributed and were not rollovers from 401(k) or other qualified employer retirement accounts. Employer plans might have superior asset protection. Consult with a lawyer who specializes in bankruptcy protection about this before going ahead with a transfer from an employer retirement account to a Roth or IRA. Maybe you should be transferring assets to the employer plan instead of the Roth or IRA!

What about inherited employer accounts? Beneficiaries must be permitted under the terms of the qualified plan to rollover the balance to a beneficiary Roth or IRA account. The IRS surprised tax advisors by explaining that rules adopted by Congress permit a direct transfer of a traditional inherited employer retirement account to a Roth account in Notice 2008-30. (Again, such a transfer would be subject to income tax.) Inherited IRA accounts can't be converted to Roth accounts.[18]

So, open your mind. You might have more investment flexibility with your retirement funds than you thought. Also, always seek competent professional advice when making financial decisions for accounts with large balances.

18 Internal Revenue Code Section 408(d)(3)(C)

13

Converting a tax deferred account to a tax-free account – at a price (Roth conversions)

The ability to convert a traditional IRA to a Roth IRA is liberal, enabling many individuals who couldn't have a Roth IRA before to have one. The rules also enable the conversion of a "regular" 401(k) account to a Roth 401(k) account. (The 401(k) plan must offer a "Roth" feature to make such a conversion.)

In the past, such a conversion wasn't allowed if your modified adjusted gross income was more than $100,000. This restriction has been eliminated.

Note that, when the taxpayer has to take required minimum distributions, the required minimum distribution must be received before a Roth conversion can be done. (See Chapter 16.)

The "price" for the conversion is the amount converted is taxable as ordinary income. The conversion is reported on Form 8606, "Nondeductible IRAs." The penalty for distributions before age 59 ½ does not apply to Roth conversions. The penalty can apply when a distribution is made from the Roth account before age 59 ½ and within five years after the conversion.

Direct conversions from qualified plan accounts (such as a 401(k) or profit sharing account) to Roth IRA accounts are also permitted. The plan must permit "in-service" distributions in order to make a conversion before retirement or separation from service.

A named beneficiary of an inherited (employer) qualified plan account may also make a direct conversion to a Roth account. Avoid an "intermediary" transfer of an inherited employer plan account to a regular inherited IRA, because that will disqualify the conversion.

Conversions of inherited regular IRAs to inherited Roth IRAs aren't permitted.

Here are four reasons for considering converting a regular IRA or retirement account balance to a Roth during 2025:

1. **<u>The Medicare (net investment income) tax.</u>** An additional 3.8% tax on net investment income, including most taxable long-term capital gains, became effective in 2013. The tax applies to individuals with modified adjusted gross income exceeding $200,000 for singles, $250,000 for married persons filing joint returns, and $125,000 for married persons filing separate returns.

This tax does not apply to distributions from retirement accounts, but will apply to earnings from reinvested distributions. There are no required distributions for a Roth IRA account during the original owner's lifetime, but there are after the original owner's death. (See Chapter 19.)

Taxable distributions from regular IRAs could increase a taxpayer's adjusted gross income, subjecting investment income to the net investment income tax.

Since Roth distributions aren't taxable, they won't increase a taxpayer's adjusted gross income and subject investment income to the net investment income tax.

(The net investment income tax was adopted as part of the Affordable Care Act of 2010 (ACA), nicknamed "Obamacare." The Tax Cuts and Jobs Act of 2017 eliminated the penalty for failure to have health insurance, effective after December 31, 2018. In 2012, the U.S. Supreme Court ruled the ACA was constitutional based on Congress's power to assess taxes, rationalizing the penalty as a tax.[19] The U.S. Supreme Court also upheld the ACA and ruled against Texas in *California v. Texas*, where Texas claimed since the tax is zero, the ACA is unconstitutional.[20])

2. **Tax-free accumulation of earnings.** After a short waiting period, most earnings in Roth IRAs are income tax-free while accumulated in the account and when distributed. (There is an exception for unrelated business taxable income in the Roth account. It won't apply to most taxpayers. See Chapter 10.) There is a toll to pay, since the Roth conversion is taxable.

   The younger the account owner, the bigger the advantage of this tax-free accumulation. Since, for accounts of individuals deceased before January 1, 2020, an inherited account can be distributed over the beneficiary's life expectancy, this avoidance can continue for a long time after the original account owner is deceased. The younger the beneficiary, the bigger the advantage, provided the beneficiary doesn't accelerate distributions. (The SECURE Act of 2020 generally eliminated life expectancy distributions for retirement accounts that were inherited after 2019, with some exceptions. See Chapters 18 and 19.)

3. **Contingency planning for higher income tax rates.** Our federal government has been accumulating debt at record rates, including providing relief for the COVID-19 pandemic but also considering big tax cuts for the wealthy and for corporations enacted in the Tax Cuts and Jobs Act of 2017. It seems logical that federal income tax rates will eventually increase to pay the debt off. Although the tax cuts enacted in the Tax Cuts and Jobs Act of 2017 are scheduled to expire after 2025, the second

19 *National Federation of Independent Business v. Sebelius*, Supreme Court 648 F. 3d 1235, June 28, 2012

20 *California et. al. v. Texas et. al.*, Supreme Court 127 AFTR 2d. 2021-2327, June 17, 2021.

Trump administration favors extending the tax cuts. Time will tell what Congress will do. Now seems to be a good time to consider making Roth contributions and Roth conversions while "taxes are on sale!"

4. **Estate planning.** Leaving a tax-free account is a nice bequest and can be considered as an alternative to life insurance. If the beneficiary is or might be in a higher tax bracket than the donor, the family will save income taxes when the donor makes a Roth conversion. If the donor will have an estate subject to estate tax, the donor's lifetime payment of income taxes will reduce the taxable estate. Also see Chapter 18 about Estate Planning for IRAs and Roths.

You can't change your mind

Once you have made a Roth conversion, you can't "undo" it. (Note that contributions other than conversions to an IRA or a Roth can still be recharacterized up to the extended due date of an income tax return.)

You also can't change your mind when you convert a 401(k) account or 457 plan account to a Roth 401(k) or 457 account.

Using a conversion to beat Roth contribution limits

For 2024, annual Roth contributions (other than rollovers and conversions) are phased out for "modified adjusted gross income" from $146,000 to $161,000 for singles, $230,000 to $240,000 for married persons filing joint returns, and $0 to $10,000 for married persons filing separate returns. For 2025, annual Roth contributions (other than rollovers and conversions) are phased out for "modified adjusted gross income" from $150,000 to $165,000 for singles, $236,000 to $246,000 for married persons filing joint returns, and $0 to $10,000 for married persons filing separate returns. The thresholds are adjusted each year for inflation.

If you have no regular IRA accounts for previous years, you can make a $7,000 non-deductible IRA contribution for 2024 up to April 15, 2025. The same limit applies for 2025. The non-deductible IRA can then be converted to a Roth account. There may be little or no taxable income for income accumulated in the non-deductible IRA after setting it up. Effectively, the Roth contribution limits are defeated in this scenario. This tactic is called a "back-door Roth contribution."

There were rumors that Congress would outlaw "backdoor Roth conversions" in SECURE 2.0 Act of 2022. It didn't happen. Instead, Roth treatment of employer contributions in employer 401(k), 403(b), and governmental 457(b) retirement accounts were liberalized.

If you already have "regular" IRA accounts accumulated through funding with deductible contributions in prior years and/or with rollovers from qualified plans, such as 401(k) accounts, all of the IRA accounts are treated as one account when a distribution is made. This means a Roth conversion after a non-deductible contribution to a "regular" IRA will carry out taxable income attributable to deductible contributions and rollovers from all of the taxable IRA accounts.

For example, if a regular IRA previously only had tax deductible contributions and had an ending balance of $44,000, after a $6,000 non-deductible contribution was made for 2024, followed by a $6,000 Roth conversion, the basis recovery would be $6,000 (amount converted) X ($6,000 (amount converted) / ($44,000 (ending balance) + $6,000 (non-deductible contribution) = $720 basis recovery. The taxable income for the conversion would be $6,000 (amount converted) - $720 (basis recovery) = $5,280 (taxable income).

Conclusion

Since regular IRA and retirement accounts can be converted to Roths regardless of the level of income, employer contributions to employer retirement accounts may now be designated as Roth contributions (effective for employer contributions after December 29, 2022) and the same for SEPs and SIMPLE plans (effective for employer contributions for taxable years beginning after December 31, 2022), and some nondeductible IRA contributions can be converted as back-door Roth contributions, taxpayers have considerable flexibility to accumulate more funds in Roth accounts.

Now seems to be a good time to make a conversion when federal income tax rates are "on sale," considering the tax cuts for individuals enacted in the Tax Cuts and Jobs Act of 2017, even if Congress extends them after 2025. With a massively growing federal debt, it seems likely income tax rates will increase in the future.

Plan for "side effects" of a conversion, such as adjustments of premiums for Medicare and paying income taxes.

These transactions should be made under the guidance of a tax advisor who is familiar with the rules, together with a financial advisor.

14

What distributions can you take from a Roth or IRA before age 59 ½?

Individual retirement accounts

Distributions from an individual retirement account before the participant reaches age 59 ½ are subject to a 10% federal additional penalty income tax. (California has a 2.5% penalty tax.)

The 10% penalty tax doesn't apply to the following partial list of distributions:

1. Distributions made on or after the date on which the IRA owner attains age 59 ½.

2. Distributions made due to the IRA owner's death or disability.

3. Distributions that are part of a series of substantially equal periodic payments made for the IRA owner's life or the joint lives of the IRA owner and his or her beneficiary. (See below.)

4. Distributions for medical expenses in excess of the 7 ½% of adjusted gross income floor.

5. Distributions used to pay health insurance premiums to an individual after separation from employment when the individual receives unemployment compensation for 12 or more consecutive weeks. The distributions may be paid in the year the unemployment compensation was paid or the next tax year. The health insurance may be for the individual and the individual's spouse and dependents.

6. Distributions used to pay "qualified higher education expenses" of the participant, the participant's spouse, or any child or grandchild of the participant or the participant's spouse.

7. Distributions used to pay certain expenses incurred by qualified first-time homebuyers (explained below). Retroactively effective for disasters occurring on or after January 26, 2021, taxpayers who received a qualified homebuyer distribution that was used to buy or construct a principal residence in a qualified disaster, but it wasn't used because of the disaster and was received on a date 180 days before the incident period of the disaster and ending on the date 30 days after the last date of the incident period, may be repaid to the IRA during the period beginning on the first day of the qualified disaster and ending on the date which is 180 days after the applicable date for the disaster and treat the repayment as a qualified rollover.

8. Distributions due to an IRS levy on the IRA.

9. Qualified hurricane and disaster distributions (cumulative/lifetime $100,000 limit).

10. Distributions to individuals called to active military duty for more than 179 days after September 11, 2001.

11. Under the SECURE Act of 2020, effective for distributions made after December 31, 2019, distributions of up to $5,000 per birth or adoption can be made free of the 10% early distributions penalty during the one-year period beginning on the date on which a child of the individual is born or on which the legal adoption by the individual of an eligible adoptee is finalized. (An eligible adoptee is any individual, other than a child of the taxpayer's spouse, who has not reached age 18 or is physically or mentally incapable of self-support.) Taxpayers must include the name, age, and taxpayer identification number of the child or adoptee on their tax return. The distributions may be recontributed to an individual's eligible retirement plan and treated as a rollover, subject to certain requirements. Effective for distributions made after December 29, 2022, the distributions may only be recontributed within three years of the period beginning on the day after the date on which the distribution was received. (The rollover is reported on an amended income tax return for the year of the distribution.)

12. Under the Further Consolidated Appropriations Act of 2020, qualified disaster distributions are exempt from the 10% early distributions penalty. A qualified disaster distribution is made on or after the first day of the incident period of a qualified disaster and before June 20, 2020. The amount excluded from the penalty shall not exceed the excess (if any) of $100,000 over the aggregate amounts treated as qualified disaster distributions received by the individual for all prior taxable years. The limitation is applied separately for each qualified disaster. A qualified disaster distribution (up to the limitation) may be repaid to the IRA within three years and treated as a trustee-to trustee transfer. The taxable income for the distribution is reported over three taxable years beginning with the year of the distribution unless the taxpayer elects to have it 100% taxed for the year of the distribution.[21]

13. Retroactively effective for disasters occurring on or after January 26, 2021, up to $22,000 of distributions to affected individuals are exempt from the 10% early distribution penalty. The taxable income for the distribution is reported over three taxable years beginning with the year of the distribution unless the taxpayer elects to have it 100% taxed for the year of the distribution. A qualified disaster distribution (up to the limitation) may be repaid to the IRA within three years and treated as a trustee-to-trustee transfer.

14. Under the CARES Act of 2020, the early distribution penalty will be waived for up to $100,000 of distributions during 2020 to an individual (1) who

21 Further Consolidated Appropriations Act 2020, Public Law 116-94, Division Q, Title II, § 202(a)

is diagnosed with coronavirus, (2) whose spouse or dependent is diagnosed with coronavirus, or (3) who experiences financial consequences as a result of being quarantined, being furloughed or laid off or having work hours reduced due to the coronavirus crisis, being unable to work due to lack of child care due to the virus, closing or reducing hours of a business owned or operated by the individual due to the virus, or other factors as determined by the IRS.

The plan participant will designate to the plan administrator that the distribution is a coronavirus-related distribution. That designation is not binding on the IRS in the event the total distributions for the plan participant exceed $100,000.

Unless the taxpayer elects out, the income from a coronavirus-related distribution will be spread ratably over a 3-taxable year period, beginning with the distribution year (2020).

Although these distributions won't be eligible under the usual rules for rollovers or trustee-to-trustee transfers, coronavirus-related distributions from a qualified plan or an IRA may be repaid to the qualified plan or an IRA within 3 years, beginning the day after the date the distribution was received. The amount repaid will be treated as a direct trustee-to-trustee transfer within 60 days of the distribution, resulting in no gross income for the repaid amount.

Since these distributions aren't considered to be rollovers, you could have as many distributions as you wanted during 2020 treated as trustee-to-trustee transfers or have them taxed over three years, provided they qualify as coronavirus-related.

Roth conversions can also be taxed over three years under the rule, provided the distribution was coronavirus related, such as if the account owner was diagnosed with a mild case of the virus.

The IRS has issued guidance that that the taxpayer will initially report the income over the three-year period. When part or all of the distribution is repaid to the IRA, any amounts not yet reported will first be reduced by the repaid amount. If the amount repaid exceeds the amounts not yet reported, amended income tax returns should be submitted to reduce the amounts already reported. See Notice 2020-50 for details.

Distributions from inherited IRAs to a nonspouse beneficiary don't qualify for rollover treatment. (IRC § 402(c)(4), (9), § 408(d)(3)(C).) (Once a distribution is received by a nonspouse beneficiary from an inherited IRA, it can't be redeposited.) (However, a direct trustee-to-trustee transfer to a beneficiary account isn't taxable and isn't subject to the 10% penalty.)

The waiver of penalty and extended rollover provisions applied to distributions on or after January 1 and before December 31, 2020. (Evidently, distributions ON December 31, 2020 didn't qualify.)[22]

---

22 Coronavirus Aid, Relief and Economic Security Act of 2020, Public Law 116-136, § 2202(a). Notice 2020-50

15. Corrective distribution of an excess contribution and related income before the extended due date of the income tax return for which the excess contribution was made.

16. Effective for distributions made after December 31, 2023, one distribution per year of up to $1,000 may be made for emergency expenses, which are unforeseeable or immediate financial needs relating to personal or family emergency expenses. The taxpayer may repay the distribution during the three years beginning the day after the distribution was received and treat the distribution as a qualified rollover. During the period the distribution may be repaid, no additional distributions for emergency expenses will qualify for the exemption.

17. Effective for distributions made after December 31, 2023, distribution of up to the lesser of $10,000, indexed for inflation for tax years after 2024, or 50% of the participant's account within a one-year period in the case of domestic abuse by a spouse or domestic partner, such as escaping an unsafe situation. This amount may be repaid and treated as a rollover within 3 years after the day after the distribution is received.

18. Effective for distributions made after December 29, 2023, distributions made to a participant who is a terminally ill individual on or after the date the participant has been certified by a physician as having a terminal illness, with an expected life expectancy of not more than 84 months. The distributions may be repaid and treated as a rollover within 3 years after the day after a distribution is received.

19. Effective for distributions made after December 29, 2025, distributions of up to $2,500 per year to pay premiums of specified long-term care insurance contracts.

Substantially equal periodic payments

Payments can be made based on the IRS life expectancy tables used to compute required minimum distributions, recomputed annually. (See Chapter 16.)

This election can be made by individuals who need access to their IRA funds before age 59 ½ and who want to avoid penalties.

Although in most cases all IRA accounts are aggregated, this election can be made on an account-by-account basis, so the amount from which payments will be made can be segregated into a separate account.

Once the election has been made, the payments must continue annually until the later of the date the participant reaches age 59 ½ or five years have elapsed.

Qualified first-time homebuyer distributions

"Qualified first-time homebuyer distributions" are withdrawals from an IRA or Roth IRA of up to $10,000 during the participant's lifetime that are used within 120 days of withdrawal to buy, build, or rebuild a principal residence of the participant, spouse, child, or grandchild of the participant or the participant's spouse. In order to be a first-time homebuyer, the individual and the individual's spouse, if married, must not have had an ownership interest in a principal residence during a two-year period ending on the date the new home is acquired.

Roth distributions

Qualified distributions from a Roth IRA are not included in the taxpayer's gross income and are not subject to the 10% federal early withdrawal tax.

To be a qualified distribution, the distribution must satisfy a five-year holding period and meet one of the following additional requirements:

1. Made on or after the date on which the participant is age 59 ½.

2. Distribution on or after the participant's death.

3. Distribution for disability.

4. Distribution used to pay for "qualified first-time homebuyer expenses" (same as for IRAs, above).

To meet the five-year holding period, the distribution may not be made before the end of the five-tax-year period beginning with the first tax year for which the individual (or the individual's spouse) made a contribution to a Roth IRA.

There is also a special holding period rule when there was a Roth conversion. See Chapter 13.

A distribution from a Roth account that isn't a qualified distribution may be taxable under an ordering rule. Distributions are first from contributions, so distributions aren't taxable until the total amount of contributions is distributed.

Taxable distributions may be subject to the 10% federal early withdrawal tax unless they meet one of the exceptions described above for individual retirement accounts.

Spousal rollover accounts after a death

Note that a surviving spouse who converts an account inherited from his or her deceased spouse to his or her own account or rolls it over to his or her own account, not as a "beneficiary," is also subject to the above early distribution penalty and also must generally wait until age 59 ½ to avoid the early distribution penalty. It might be desirable to wait for the rollover. See Chapter 19 for more details.

15

Distributions permitted from a Roth or Traditional IRA starting age 59 ½ and before the required beginning date

Once the participant reaches age 59 ½ until the participant reaches the applicable age for determining the required beginning date, the participant has total flexibility for taking distributions from an IRA or Roth (assuming the Roth account has been open at least five years). Distributions are permitted, but not required.

Minimum distributions are required starting at age 75 for account owners of a traditional IRA who first reach age 74 after December 31, 2032, 73 for account owners who first reach age 72 after December 31, 2022 and age 73 before January 1, 2033, 72 for account owners who first reach age 70 1/2 after December 31, 2019 and age 72 before January 1, 2023, and 70 ½ for account owners who first reach age 70 ½ before 2020. This is the *applicable age*. The date when minimum distributions must begin, April 1 of the year following reaching the applicable age, is called the *required beginning date* or RBD.

See Chapter 16 about required minimum distributions when the account owner reaches the RBD.

There is a special holding period rule when there was a Roth conversion. See Chapter 13.

16

Required annual distributions during the participant's lifetime after the required beginning date

The participant (account owner) of a regular IRA reaches the *applicable age for determining the required beginning date* when they first reach --

- Age 70 ½ for account owners who first reach age 70 ½ before 2020

- Age 72 for account owners who first reach
  - Age 70 ½ after December 31, 2019 and
  - Age 72 before January 1, 2023

- Age 73 for account owners who first reach
  - Age 72 after December 31, 2022 and
  - Age 73 before January 1, 2033

- Age 75 after December 31, 2032 for account owners who first reach age 74 after December 31, 2032.

The *required beginning date* (RBD) is April 1 of the taxable year following the year the participant reaches the applicable age. Distributions are generally required to be made by December 31 each year, with the exception of the year the account owner reaches the applicable age. The participant has the option to take the distribution for that year by the RBD. In that case, there will be two distributions that year, one by April 1 and another by December 31. Otherwise, the participant may take a required minimum distribution by December 31 of the year the applicable age was reached and a required minimum distribution by December 31 of the following year. The choice might matter if the lower income tax brackets are otherwise unused. A present value analysis may be helpful in that regard. See below for details about computation of required minimum distributions.

Reminder – required minimum distributions must be received before a taxpayer can make a rollover or a Roth conversion. (See Chapters 12 and 13.)

To avoid missing a required minimum distribution, consider scheduling automatic distributions with the account custodian.

See the explanation of Qualified Charitable Distributions in Chapter 6. Qualified Charitable Distributions "count" as distributions for the required minimum distributions test.

There are no required minimum distributions for a Roth IRA account during the lifetime of the participant/account owner. Beneficiaries who inherit a Roth IRA account have different rules. See Chapter 19 about handling IRA and Roth accounts after a death.

Effective for tax years beginning after December 31, 2023, Roth accounts in a 401(k) or other employer retirement plan also don't have required minimum distributions during the participant's lifetime. Before 2024, Roth 401(k) accounts did have required minimum distributions. This was a reason for rolling a Roth 401(k) account to a Roth IRA account upon retirement. Those employer-sponsored Roth accounts that were making required distributions before 2024 can discontinue them after 2023, except the payment due April 1, 2024 for plan participants who reach the applicable age for required minimum distributions during 2023 was still required.

Effective December 29, 2022, the participant may elect to aggregate distributions for the portion of the account holding an annuity and the rest of the account for computing requirement minimum distributions. (Most aren't annuitized.)

When the participant doesn't make this election and an IRA or Roth is annuitized, the annuitized account handled separately from other IRAs. Distributions are made according to an annuity schedule that will be handled by the insurance company.

The IRS has issued final regulations relating to computing required minimum distributions when an IRA includes annuitized benefits and non-annuitized benefits.[23] When the election to aggregate isn't made, it's much simpler to just have separate accounts for each.

Effective for calendar years ending after December 29, 2022, IRAs are allowed to own commercial annuities incorporating annuity payments that increase by a constant percentage of up to 5% per year and other provisions. Congress's intention was to provide more annuity investment alternatives for IRA owners.

Another option for IRAs is to invest in a "Qualified Longevity Annuity Contract," or QLAC. The purpose of a QLAC is to postpone the date when retirement payments are required to begin so that participants don't outlive their retirement savings. The QLAC is excluded from the required minimum distribution computations until payments under the contract commence. These contracts provide life annuity payments beginning at an advanced age (no later than the first day of the month following the 85th birthday of the participant). Effective for contracts purchased or received in an exchange after December 29, 2022, the limit of premiums invested in QLACs for a participant is $200,000. The $200,000 limit will be indexed for inflation for calendar years beginning on or after January 1, 2024. For 2024, the limit is $200,000. For 2025, the limit is $210,000. A previous limitation of 25% of the participant's account balance on the date of the payment has been repealed. Effective for contracts purchased or received in an exchange on or after July 14, 2014, account owners who purchase a QLAC have a "free look" period of up to 90 days after the transaction to have it rescinded. Effective for contracts purchased or received in an exchange on or after July 14, 2014, the survivor rights under a joint and survivor annuity purchased as a QLAC will be preserved after a divorce.

The distribution is usually computed by dividing the account balance at the end of the previous year by an applicable distribution period from the Uniform Lifetime Table. (The table is included in Appendix B at the end of this book.) You look up the period based on

23 Treasury Regulations § 1.401(a)(9)-5(a)(5)

the participant's age at the end of the year. For example, if Jane will be age 73 at the end of 2024 and her account balance was $265,000 at the end of 2023, her required distribution for 2024 will be $265,000 / 26.5 = $10,000.

Notice that the applicable distribution period factor is not reduced by one each year. There is a recalculation of life expectancy, which is extended for each year the participant survives. That illustrates that, according to actuarial tables, the longer you *do* live, the longer you *will* live.

The table includes an extended life expectancy for an assumed beneficiary who is ten years younger than the participant, even if the account has no named beneficiary. (This has nothing to do with the 10-year rule that generally applies to designated beneficiaries of inherited Roth and IRA accounts who are not Eligible Designated Beneficiaries.)

There is an exception when the sole beneficiary of the IRA account is the spouse of the participant and the spouse is more than ten years younger than the participant. There is a special Joint and Last Survivor Table used to determine the applicable distribution period in that case, which you can find in Publication 590B. The calculation process is similar, except you use the factor from the other table, using the ages for both spouses. The standard dual-life table is used even if a charity is named as the primary beneficiary of the account.

Under the required minimum distribution rules, all of the participant's IRA accounts held as the *owner* are treated as one. (Inherited IRA accounts are handled separately. See Chapter 19 about handling IRA and Roth accounts after a death.) The required distribution is computed based on the total account balances (excluding annuitized amounts, unless aggregation is elected) at the end of the previous year. The distribution can be withdrawn from one or a combination of accounts.

When computing the account balance as of the end of the previous year, you must increase the balance for any IRA rollovers that haven't been completed by the year-end.[24]

The account balance is not reduced for a required minimum distribution for the year that is paid the next year, when the participant reached the applicable age for determining the required beginning date. (This is a minor disadvantage of postponing payment until the next year.)

Effective for taxable years beginning after December 29, 2022, the penalty for failure to make a required minimum distribution is 25% of the undistributed amount and might be reduced to 10% if the participant timely receives a corrective distribution. Before 2023, the penalty was 50% of the undistributed amount. In addition to required payments on or after the required beginning date, penalties can apply for a series of substantially equal payments before age 59 ½ and for inherited retirement accounts. (The taxpayer can still request a waiver of penalties for a "reasonable cause.") Any formal change in the regulations would likely only apply to future years.

SECURE 2.0 Act of 2022 extends the Employee Plans Compliance Resolution System to IRAs and Roth IRAs, providing procedures to correct failures resulting in a penalty. See Chapter 7 for more details.

---

24 Treasury Regulations § 1.401(a)(9)-7, A-2

The IRS has issued final regulations relating to required minimum distributions from retirement accounts, including 401(k), IRA and Roth IRA accounts.[25] The final regulations are effective for retirement plan distributions for tax years beginning on or after January 1, 2022. Additional final regulations and proposed regulations were issued July 19, 2024, effective for determining required minimum distributions for calendar years beginning on or after January 1, 2025.[26]

25 TD 9930, November 12, 2020; Treasury Regulations Section 1.401(a)(9)-9

26 TD 10001 and REG-103529-23

17
Valuation and retirement accounts

As in many areas of taxation, valuation is a key issue for retirement accounts. However, there is surprisingly little guidance about how valuation should be applied, so valuation is a neglected issue and can be viewed as "the elephant in the room" that few people talk about.

Required minimum distributions are computed based on the "account balance at the beginning of the year".[27] Evidently, the author of the regulations was thinking of retirement accounts like a bank account - a nice, simple cash figure. IRS Publications 590A and 590B on IRAs also describes the IRA account balance as "the amount in the IRA at the end of the year preceding the year for which the required minimum distribution is being figured".

IRA and Roth custodians are required to report the account balance as of the end of the year at line 5 of Form 5498 so the account owner can compute the required minimum distribution for a taxable year, if applicable.

Most retirement plan administrators will annually revalue assets that are easy to value, such as marketable securities, certificates of deposit and bank accounts. In the past, they have typically used the cost of hard-to-value assets, such as partnership interests or corporate stock that isn't publicly traded, when computing the "fair market value" or "account balance." In addition, accrued but unpaid dividends and interest are disregarded for computing the account balance. This is a practical convenience.

The IRS has awakened to this issue. Effective for 2015, the IRS requires the separate disclosure of the fair market value of specified assets, including stock of corporations that aren't publicly traded, partnership and LLC interests that aren't publicly traded, private mortgages, real estate, non-traded options, and other assets that don't have a readily available fair market value.[28] This information is reported at boxes 15a and 15b of Form 5498. The instructions for Form 5498 simply state that the fair market value is required to be disclosed with no explanation about how it should be determined.

"Fair market value" (FMV) is a loaded description for tax reporting. It represents the amount an informed buyer would pay an informed seller, neither being under any obligation to engage in a sale or exchange transaction. How you compute FMV has grown into a huge industry, involving "valuation adjustments" for lack of marketability and/or minority interests. Having a business valuation study done for business interests that aren't publicly traded costs thousands of dollars. An appraisal may only be a starting point for determining the fair market value. There may be additional accruals to be considered. Volumes have been written about fair market value. A detailed discussion is beyond the scope of this book.

Rules for computing the value for annuity contracts held inside a defined contribution plan for required minimum distribution purposes are explained at Treasury Regulations § 1.401(a)(9)-6(m). The details are beyond the scope of this discussion. The method may not

27 Treasury Regulations § 1.401(a)(9)-5(b)
28 2024 Instructions for Forms 1099-R and 5498, pages 20 and 22

be used to value a contract for a Roth IRA conversion. See Treasury Regulations § 1.408A-4, A-14 for annuity contracts distributed in Roth conversions.

If an account balance is understated, the required minimum distribution could be understated, potentially exposing the account owner to a penalty. Effective for taxable years beginning after December 29, 2022, the penalty for failure to make a required minimum distribution is 25% of the undistributed amount and might be reduced to 10% if the participant timely receives a corrective distribution. Before 2023, the penalty was 50% of the undistributed amount.

In addition to required payments on or after the required beginning date (see Chapter 16), penalties can apply for failure to make a payment in a series of substantially equal payments before age 59 ½ and for failure to make required distributions for inherited retirement accounts (see Chapter 19).

In the years when no distributions are made or required to be made and there is no Roth conversion, the FMV has no tax consequence. The IRS hasn't stated any consequences of misstating the FMV on Form 5498 in this scenario.

The value on box 5 of Form 5498 can't be used for estate tax reporting. The underlying assets must be valued for that purpose.[29] However, the instructions for Form 5498 now give the plan custodian the option of reporting the date of death or the year-end value for the account on Form 5498 issued to the decedent. According to the instructions, the year-end value will probably be zero because a Form 5498 should be issued to the beneficiary(ies) of the account with the year-end balance(s). (The year-end value will be zero if the account is distributed to the beneficiaries by the year-end. That might not be the case. See Chapter 19.)

As I understand it, custodians of self-directed Roth and IRA accounts rely on the account owner or the asset sponsor of the investment to provide the fair market value amounts that they report on Form 5498, which are needed from many non-traditional investments. The account owner is responsible for obtaining and paying for any required appraisals. The cost for getting an appraisal of most residential real estate isn't very great, but the cost to appraise a business or other real estate may be prohibitive and lead to the decision to avoid many alternative investments.

In one case, famed actor James Caan, who played Sonny Corleone in *The Godfather* and was in many other motion pictures and television shows, failed to provide the fair market value of a hedge fund to the custodian of his IRA for 2014, in violation of the custodial agreement. (James Caan didn't manage his business affairs himself; he had professional managers.) The custodian, Union Bank of Switzerland (UBS) distributed the hedge fund during 2015 and issued Form 1099R reporting the last fair market value received for 2013, $1,910,903.

James Caan's wealth management advisor left UBS during 2015 and joined Merrill Lynch. Merrill Lynch's Automated Customer Account Transfer Service wouldn't accept the hedge fund, so the wealth manager ordered the liquidation of the hedge fund for $1,532,605.46, and deposited the proceeds in James Caan's new IRA at Merrill Lynch. The sale and deposit didn't take place until almost a year after UBS notified James Caan that it

29 Treasury Regulations § 20.2031(b)(1)

had distributed the hedge fund. The assets in James Caan's other UBS IRAs were directly transferred to his IRA at Merrill Lynch at the same time.

James Caan reported the distribution as a nontaxable rollover on his 2015 income tax return.

The IRS notified James Caan the transactions didn't qualify as a rollover because the 60-day requirement wasn't met, and assessed additional income taxes and an accuracy-related penalty.

James Caan's representatives requested a private letter ruling extending the time for completing the rollover and filed a petition for him in Tax Court on July 30, 2018. (He died July 6, 2022.)

The IRS denied the extension, and pointed out James Caan failed another requirement for a qualified rollover. The same property received must be deposited to the new IRA.

On October 18, 2023, the Tax Court ruled in favor of the IRS, that the transfer was taxable for 2015, because it didn't qualify as a rollover due to the sale of the hedge fund before depositing the proceeds to the new IRA and the transfer wasn't completed within 60 days after the distribution. In addition, the Court used an updated valuation provided by the IRS based on the ending capital account balance on the hedge fund's Schedule K-1 for tax year 2015, $1,548,010.[30]

If the hedge fund had been sold inside the UBS IRA before the distribution and rollover to the Merrill Lynch IRA, the IRS might have extended the 60-day deadline and eliminated this mess.

Since the transfer didn't qualify as a rollover, it was also an excess contribution to James Caan's IRA, subject to an annual 6% federal tax penalty until the amount is distributed from the account. This issue wasn't raised in the Tax Court decision

30 *Estate of James Caan v. Commissioner*, 161 TC No. 6, October 18, 2023

18

Estate Planning for IRAs and Roths

The details of estate planning are beyond the scope of this book. You should seek the help of a qualified team of professionals, including an attorney, life insurance agent, tax advisor, financial planner and others.

For most individuals, their retirement accounts represent a major asset. The two major asset classes for most people are their home and their retirement accounts.

On the other hand, retirement accounts are somewhat "invisible" because we don't have regular access to them. They are sometimes neglected in estate planning – a huge mistake.

The SECURE Act of 2019 has radically changed the rules of the game for inherited retirement accounts for nonspouse beneficiaries, effective for deaths after 2019. SECURE Act 2.0, enacted December 29, 2022, also includes some provisions that should be studied for the estate plans of plan participants. The IRS issued final regulations implementing the SECURE Act of 2019 and the SECURE 2.0 Act of 2022 and proposed regulations for some provisions of the SECURE 2.0 Act of 2022 on July 19, 2024.[31] Everyone who has a retirement account with a significant balance, including inherited beneficiary accounts, should meet with an estate planning attorney and a tax consultant who have studied these rules. You will not be able to develop as good of a plan as you could before the SECURE Acts were enacted and will have to cobble something together the best you can. We explore some alternatives at the end of this chapter. Your plan will probably have to be updated again for any future tax law changes.

Another wild card is the temporary increase of the estate and gift tax exemption by the Tax Cuts and Jobs Act of 2017. The estate and gift tax exemption has been doubled from $5 million to $10 million, indexed for inflation after 2010, effective for tax years beginning after 2017 and expiring for tax years after 2025. The exemption equivalent is $13,610,000 for 2024 and $13,990,000 for 2025. Under the current federal estate tax laws, the estate tax exemption is "portable" for surviving spouses. This means the unused exemption for the last-deceased spouse can be available for the surviving spouse, enabling a married couple to have a combined taxable estate of up to $27,220,000 for 2024 or $27,980,000 for 2025 and not be subject to estate tax.

The exemption increase is scheduled to expire after 2025. The IRS has issued guidance for what will happen after 2025 to exemptions increased using portability elections made by estates of decedents who died before 2026. The exemption of the deceased spouse that is ported to the surviving spouse is not reduced after 2025 and will generally be available for the surviving spouse if the surviving spouse qualifies (the account owner was the last deceased spouse of the surviving spouse).[32] Certain transfers won't be eligible for this "anti-clawback" protection when gifts made before 2026 aren't "true" lifetime transfers, such as for retained

31 TD 10001 and REG-103529-23

32 Treasury Regulations §§ 20.2010-1(c) and 20.2010-3(a)

interests and life estates.[33]

The second Trump administration says it intends to extend the tax cuts in the Tax Cuts and Jobs Act of 2017, so estate planning for a reduced estate tax exemption seems less urgent. There can be no assurance about what Congress will ultimately do.

After the 2024 Presidential election is over, members of Congress will work on tax reform during 2025.

For individuals with estates well below the higher exemptions, the emphasis of estate planning has shifted from estate and gift taxes to income taxes. For 2024, trusts are now subject to the maximum federal income tax rate of 37% when their taxable income exceeds $15,200. For 2025, the threshold is $15,650. The 3.8% net investment income tax, in addition to the federal income tax, also applies for trusts when their income exceeds $15,200 for 2024 and $15,650 for 2025. (The 3.8% net investment income tax was enacted in the Affordable Care Act of 2010, which, so far, has been upheld by the U.S. Supreme Court.)

The tax basis of certain assets (excluding retirement accounts, which are considered "income with respect of a decedent") that are included in the taxable estate of a decedent is adjusted to fair market value on the date of death, sometimes called a "stepped-up basis," although it can also be "stepped down." Estate plans are being designed to avoid "bypass" strategies and include appreciated family assets in modest estates, including the use of qualified terminable interest property (QTIP) trusts. Depending on what Congress does for tax years beginning after 2025, bypass trusts might become popular again.

In addition, the various states have different inheritance tax regimes and differences in their laws for transferring property that will require attention from a local attorney.

Here are some estate planning tips for a Roth IRA or regular IRA.

(Note relating to the following discussion: required minimum distributions were suspended for 2020 under the CARES Act as a COVID-19 relief measure. There was no required minimum distribution for 2020. Despite the distribution being suspended, the required beginning date (RBD) is still used for other purposes. In addition, the IRS has waived penalties for failing to make required minimum distributions (RMDs) from some retirement accounts inherited by individuals after the required beginning date for 2021 through 2024.[34] No make-up distributions apply for distributions made for those years, but they are still RMD amounts that aren't eligible for rollovers to other retirement accounts. For example, undistributed RMDs for 2021 – 2024 of an inherited 401(k) account aren't eligible for a rollover to an inherited IRA.)

Do wills or trusts govern disposition of the account?

IRAs and Roths are contractual accounts, which means their disposition generally isn't controlled by a will or trust, but by beneficiary designations by the account owner. A trust can be named as a beneficiary, but this should be done carefully or the tax deferral for the account can be lost.

33 Proposed Treasury Regulations § 20.2010-1(c)(3).
34 IRS Notices 2022-53, 2023-54, and 2024-35

Generally, an estate should never be named as the beneficiary for an IRA or Roth. A trust under a will, called a testamentary trust, or a stand-alone trust are better alternatives than an estate.

A will or trust will control the disposition of the account if the estate or trust is the beneficiary of the account. There are a host of consequences from making an estate or trust the beneficiary, some of which are discussed in this chapter and Chapter 19. Making an estate or trust the beneficiary should not be done lightly, and then only with the counsel of a qualified lawyer and a qualified tax advisor.

When a beneficiary is a minor, is disabled, or otherwise needs professional management of the assets in a retirement account, a trust probably should be named as a beneficiary of the account.

Beneficiaries who receive benefits from Medicaid (including MediCal) could have their benefits reduced when they receive distributions from an inherited retirement account. The owner of the account should consult with their attorney about making a special-needs trust the beneficiary of the retirement account.

Some families prefer to have a "family pot" trust where distributions are made according to the beneficiaries' needs. Retirement accounts aren't the ideal assets for funding that type of trust. If there aren't enough other assets available, I suggest using life insurance, possibly held in an irrevocable life insurance trust, as an alternative. See your estate planning attorney.

Note that, if a beneficiary form isn't in effect (hasn't been signed and submitted), the plan document or IRA adoption agreement will specify who the beneficiary will be. For qualified (employer) plans, the beneficiary will typically be the surviving spouse. For IRAs, the beneficiary will typically be the estate. IRA providers are inconsistent about this. As part of the estate planning process, study the plan document.

ERISA joint and survivor annuity requirements

Employer retirement plans other than single employer plans must provide that the benefit will be a qualified joint and survivor annuity. This requirement can be waived. The spouse of the account owner should seek legal counsel about whether a waiver is desirable.

Community property

In community property states, the account owner's spouse may have enforceable rights in the account. If the participant is married and the beneficiary is someone other than the participant's spouse, the spouse may be entitled to compensation when the account goes to the named beneficiary. Consult with legal counsel about the rights of each spouse. If ERISA applies (the federal law for employer retirement plans), the terms of that law will be controlling. ERISA doesn't apply for IRAs or Roth IRAs.

Therefore, a married participant/account owner should get the written consent of his or her spouse, including a valid community property transmutation agreement, if a beneficiary other than the spouse is named. A valid and enforceable transmutation agreement should be prepared with legal guidance, and each spouse should have their own legal counsel. The beneficiary designation must conform with the transmutation agreement. If the participant doesn't get written consent from his or her spouse when the spouse isn't named as the beneficiary, the spouse should get legal advice about how to deal with the situation.

Spouse as sole beneficiary

In most cases, you can get the maximum deferral for the account and achieve the maximum flexibility by naming your spouse as the sole beneficiary. The reason is the surviving spouse has the option of converting the account to his or her own IRA or Roth IRA. For accounts inherited before 2020, most beneficiaries have to compute required distributions using a single life table. See below for the 10-year distribution rule for accounts inherited after 2019 (surviving spouses are generally exempt from that rule). Surviving spouses who convert or roll inherited IRAs to their own accounts can compute required distributions using the Uniform Lifetime Table, based on a joint life expectancy with an assumed beneficiary who is 10 years younger. (But surviving spouses who are less than age 59 ½ shouldn't convert too soon or should consider a partial rollover. See Chapter 19 on handling IRAs and Roths after a death, including the new election effective for calendar years beginning after December 31, 2023 to treat the surviving spouse as the deceased account owner at item 6.) Other special benefits may also be available when the spouse is named as the sole beneficiary for a Roth or IRA account.

With changes enacted in the SECURE Act, surviving spouses inheriting very large retirement accounts and who don't need them might consider making a partial or complete disclaimer of an inherited account to spread the benefits to more beneficiaries and reduce the income tax burden for the family. See the discussion at the end of this chapter and in Chapter 19.

Surviving spouses who convert an inherited Roth account to their own aren't required to take distributions during their lifetimes.

Employer plan supersedes distribution rules

Some employer plans state distribution dates earlier than those required by the IRS. In those cases, the plan will supersede the IRS rules. To avoid having to make earlier distributions, consider rolling the account to an inherited IRA or Roth account.

QTIP Trusts

Most states have a Uniform Principal and Income Act defining how much of a distribution received by a trust is principal and how much is income. Qualified Terminable Interest Property (QTIP) trusts are designed to qualify for the federal estate tax marital deduction. The trust income is required to be distributed to the surviving spouse each year. If the retirement account provides information about the internal income of the fund to the trustee, the trustee must determine whether the internal income should be distributable as such. In other words, the amount to distribute for the plan may be the greater of the required minimum distribution or the income of the account. Amounts of income determined by activity of the account can be distributed as income to the beneficiary. The trust distribution in excess of the accounting income may be retained by the trust, subject to high income tax rates for trusts.[35]

According to the IRS, both the retirement plan benefit and the trust must meet the marital deduction requirements.[36] According to Revenue Ruling 2000-2 (modified and superseded by Revenue Ruling 2006-26), the governing instrument requirements are satisfied for a retirement benefit payable to a marital trust if (1) the marital trust contains the required language, giving the spouse the right to all the trust's and the plan's income annually and (2) the retirement plan document doesn't have any provisions that would prevent the trustee of the QTIP trust from complying with the trust's provisions for the plan.

QTIP trusts generally are not an ideal beneficiary for a retirement plan. It may be better to develop an alternative approach. The retirement account benefits are distributed over the single life expectancy of the oldest trust beneficiary, usually the surviving spouse. As a result, there is substantially less deferral than would be available if the spouse was the outright sole beneficiary of the account and rolled over the benefits to his or her own account. There may be other factors that would lead to deciding to designate a QTIP trust as a beneficiary. Consult with your legal counsel about this.

Note that no spousal rollover is allowed when the IRA is owned by a QTIP trust because the account isn't owned by the surviving spouse.

Also note that, under applicable state law, a trust might be able to define "Income" to mean a unitrust amount, for example, "4 percent of the value of the account valued as of the beginning of each calendar year".

Named beneficiaries

If the participant/owner dies after 2019 and before the required beginning date (see Chapter 16), and the account has a named beneficiary, the account generally must be distributed by the end of the tenth year after the death of the participant.

Note that, effective for tax years ending after December 31, 2023, Roths in an employer's retirement plan don't have a required beginning date. Before then, those Roths had the same required beginning date as other (non-Roth) retirement accounts. (The required minimum distribution due April 1, 2024 still was required to be paid for participants who reached the applicable age for required minimum distributions during 2023.) There is an exception for an employer account that includes a designated Roth account, or DRAC. The computation for RMDs when the plan participant dies after the required beginning date *includes the DRAC account balance.*[37]

When the beneficiary for the account isn't an individual (such as an estate or a charity) and the participant died before the required beginning date, the account is required to be distributed by December 31 of the year that includes the fifth anniversary of the death of the plan participant. (This five-year rule hasn't changed under the SECURE Act.)

35 California Probate Code Section 16361, generally effective January 1, 2010
36 Revenue Rulings 2006-26, 2006-22, and 2000-2
37 Treasury Regulations Section 1.401(a)(9)-5(b)(3).

When the participant died on or after the required beginning date and the beneficiary isn't an individual, required minimum distributions are made at least as rapidly as during the participant's life, computed using the participant's remaining life ("ghost life expectancy"), determined using the single life table, with the factor reduced by one for each successive year. This rule was not changed by the SECURE Act of 2019 or the final regulations implementing the Act.

For participants deceased before January 1, 2020, if the beneficiary for the account is an individual (other than a surviving spouse) or a qualifying trust, the account is distributed based on the beneficiary's single actuarial life, or the participant's actuarial life, whichever is longer, using the single life table. (See Chapter 19 on handling an IRA or Roth account after a death.) See below for participants deceased after December 31, 2019. If the surviving spouse is the sole beneficiary, the spouse can make a rollover to his or her own account, making the spouse the owner going forward. Also see the explanation under *spouse as sole beneficiary*, above, about surviving spouses' election to treat themselves as the plan participant of an inherited employer account.

Effective for participants deceased after December 31, 2019 *and for successor beneficiaries (even when the account was originally inherited before 2020) when the previous beneficiary died after December 31, 2019*, the balance in the retirement account (that isn't subject to the five-year distribution requirement) must generally be distributed within 10 years after the date of death. See below about eligible designated beneficiaries.

There was a surprise for some in the early 2022 proposed regulations implementing the SECURE Act and confirmed in final regulations issued July 19, 2024. For participants deceased after December 31, 2019 who died after the required beginning date (see Chapter 16), required minimum distributions to most designated beneficiaries must be made for the first nine years after death computed using the greater of the designated beneficiary's life expectancy or the (deceased) participant's life expectancy. The balance of the account is distributed during the tenth year after the death of the participant. This rule recognizes that, where death occurs on or after the participant's required beginning date, the SECURE Act did not change the pre-SECURE Act rule requiring that distributions after death must be made at least as rapidly as during a lifetime.

There are some exceptions for individuals who qualify as "eligible designated beneficiaries." Here is a list of those who qualify.

1. The surviving spouse of the participant. See Chapter 19, item 6. Under a deemed election, a surviving spouse beneficiary has required minimum distributions computed using the Uniform Life Table, recalculated each year. (Look up the age on the table each year to get the factor.) The distributions begin on the *later* of the year after the participant's death or the year the participant would have reached the age for which the required beginning date applies. (See Chapter 16.) Also, the surviving spouse is eligible to rollover the account or designate the account as their own.

2. When a minor child (under age 21) of the participant is the beneficiary of the account, it can be distributed using the single life expectancy table, using the age of the beneficiary the year after the death of the participant, reduced by one for

each subsequent year, with the balance paid out the tenth year after the beneficiary reaches age 21. (Note this exception does not apply to grandchildren, only to minor children of the participant.)

3. Certain disabled beneficiaries. Required minimum distributions start the year after the decedent's date of death. When the participant died before the required beginning date, the beneficiary might be able to elect to use the 10-year distribution rule, with no distribution required until the tenth year after the participant's death. Otherwise, required minimum distributions begin the year after the participant's death. When the participant died before the required beginning date, the required minimum distribution is computed for the beneficiary's life expectancy using the single life table for the year after death, reduced by one for each subsequent year. When the participant died after the required beginning date, the greater of the life expectancy of the decedent or the beneficiary for the year after death is used, reduced by one for each subsequent year, with the balance distributed no later than the year the life expectancy of the beneficiary would have been one or less. *(In that case, the distribution period for older beneficiaries could be less than ten years.)* (The same procedure applied before the SECURE Act of 2019, without the 10-year distribution option.)

4. Chronically ill beneficiaries. Same as for disabled beneficiaries.

5. Other beneficiaries who are not more than 10 years younger than the participant. Same as for disabled beneficiaries.

Note that after an eligible designated beneficiary's death, required minimum distributions continue based on the remaining life expectancy schedule of the eligible designated beneficiary, with the balance distributed during the year that includes the tenth anniversary of the eligible designated beneficiary's death.

In the past, if the family wanted to extend the distribution period for the account, individual beneficiaries would generally be named for IRA and Roth accounts. Having a qualified beneficiary still extends the distribution period from five years to ten years.

A trust can be a qualified beneficiary, entitled to the single actuarial life, for accounts inherited before 2020, if all of the beneficiaries can be determined on the date of death and all of the beneficiaries are individuals. For accounts inherited before 2020, the applicable distribution period is determined based on the life expectancy of the oldest trust beneficiary for the year after the death of the participant. For accounts inherited after 2019, the account must be distributed within 10 years after the death of the participant unless all of the beneficiaries are eligible designated beneficiaries. When one of the beneficiaries of the trust is a minor child of the account owner, the account must be distributed the earlier of within ten years after the date the youngest child reaches age 21 or ten years after that child's death. (Note that under the 2022 proposed regulations, it was the oldest child.)

The distribution is made to the trust, and the trust may make distributions to the beneficiaries, carrying out taxable income, or accumulate undistributed amounts, subjecting them to income taxes at the trust's high federal income tax rates. Note that a portion of the distribution would be principal under fiduciary accounting rules and might not be distributable for some trusts. Alternatively, the trust instrument can specify that all retirement plan distributions should be classified as income.

As explained in Chapter 19, required minimum distributions for an account inherited from a decedent who died before 2020 with multiple beneficiaries generally are computed based on the age of the oldest beneficiary.

If the beneficiary of a retirement account is a trust that distributes to one or more other trusts, all of those trusts are tested as if they were one combined trust.[38]

If a trust is named as the beneficiary on the beneficiary designation form that is required by its terms to divide into separate trusts following the grantor's death, the separate trusts are called subtrusts. If the separate subtrusts are NOT named separately on the beneficiary designation form, you must test all of the subtrusts collectively as one trust, unless the trust meets certain requirements. (The final regulations issued July 19, 2024 change the rules for Applicable Multi-Beneficiary Trusts (AMBTs) from the 2022 proposed regulations. It is now possible for subtrusts to qualify for separate accounts treatment for RMDs, even if there are no disabled or chronically ill beneficiaries.)

For separate account treatment, under the terms of the funding trust, the funding trust must be "divided immediately upon the death of the employee" into separate see-through trusts (trusts with only individuals as "countable" beneficiaries.)[39] Administrative delays don't violate the requirement provided amounts received during the administrative period are allocated as if the trust were divided on the date of the account owner's death. Separate accounts treatment will NOT be allowed when a trust divides into subtrusts unless the share of each subtrust is fixed in the trust instrument.[40] Name the retirement account and percentage for each subtrust. That requirement mimics the requirement of naming the subtrust in the beneficiary designation form. No discretion in allocating the account is permitted. If the trust instrument has a "pick and choose" funding provision, make sure retirement benefits are excepted from that provision.

When the separate shares or subtrusts are named directly as separate beneficiaries on the beneficiary designation form, those trusts are tested separately. (Since the subtrust itself is the beneficiary, Reg. § 1.401(a)(9)-4(f)(4) doesn't apply.)

(In most cases, it will be best to name the subtrusts as separate beneficiaries on the beneficiary designation form.)

Since the ten-year distribution requirement will apply to most of these accounts inherited after 2019, separation won't be necessary unless one or more of the beneficiaries are minors or other eligible designated beneficiaries. Beneficiaries will probably still prefer separate accounts so they, or a trustee, can decide when to take distributions exceeding RMDs from their own accounts.

If one of multiple beneficiaries for an account is not an individual, such as a charity, that share will have to be paid off by September 30 of the year after death or the account will have to be distributed within five years after death in the "death before required beginning date" scenario, or using the remaining life of the deceased account owner in the "death on

38 Treasury regulations section 1.401(a)(9)-4(f)(4).
39 Treasury regulations section 1.401(a)(9)-8(a)(1)(iii)(B).
40 Treasury regulations section 1.401(a)(9)-8(a)(1)(iii)(C).

or after the required beginning date" scenario. (This rule is unchanged by the SECURE Act.) See below about when the charity won't be "counted" as a beneficiary. Effective for calendar years beginning after December 29, 2022, a special needs trust for a disabled beneficiary won't be subject to the five-year distribution requirement when it has a charitable organization as the remainder beneficiary.

Under final regulations issued by the IRS to implement the SECURE Act for years after 2019, trusts with multiple tiers of beneficiaries may have a non-individual beneficiary at the third tier and not be subject to the five-year distribution rule. Only the first- and second-tier beneficiaries are "counted" for determining required minimum distributions.

When the first-tier beneficiary of a trust is a minor child and that child will receive his share outright by age 31, any beneficiaries who would benefit from the account only if that child dies *before* reaching age 31 are disregarded.[41]

Another exception for years after 2019 applies when the trust is a "conduit trust". Only the first-tier beneficiary is "counted" for determining required minimum distributions (generally by the tenth year after the death of the participant).

For accounts inherited from a decedent who died before 2020, if the participant died on or after the required beginning date, the minimum required distribution for non-individual beneficiaries is the remaining (single life table) actuarial life of the beneficiary. For accounts inherited from an account beneficiary who died before 2020, the required minimum distribution is based on the remaining actuarial life for the beneficiary who originally inherited the account. This is usually better than the five-year distribution requirement that applies when the participant dies before the required beginning date, but an even better result would usually apply with a named individual beneficiary.

For accounts inherited from a decedent who died after 2020 or from a beneficiary who inherited an account before 2020, the ten-year distribution rule will apply in most cases, unless all of the beneficiaries are eligible designated beneficiaries or another exception applies.

Note that when a trust has multiple beneficiaries who are minor children of the account owner who are first-tier beneficiaries, the age of the oldest beneficiary controls the life expectancy. The single life table for the oldest child will be used to make required minimum distributions, subtracting one for each subsequent year. The balance of the account must be distributed by the year the *youngest* beneficiary reaches age 31. If the youngest beneficiary dies before reaching age 31, the balance of the account must be distributed when there are no minor child beneficiaries who are older than age 31.[42] (Under the 2022 proposed regulations, the age of the *oldest* beneficiary controlled the final distribution of the account.)

See Chapter 19 for more details about required minimum distributions after the death of the participant.

The estate planning team should carefully review the beneficiary designations for each retirement account and trust. In some cases, the participant should consider segregating shares before death to avoid an inadvertent result after death. Another option is to form a trust that includes provisions creating a subtrust for each individual beneficiary, and then

41 Treasury Regulations Section 1.401(a)(9)-4(f)(3)(ii)(B)
42 Treasury Regulations Section 1.401(a)(9)-5(f)(2)(ii)(C)

name each subtrust as the beneficiary of a share of the retirement account on the account beneficiary form.

Important for individual named beneficiaries

When a named beneficiary who is an individual predeceases the account owner, his or her name is treated as a "blank." If no other contingent beneficiaries are named, his or her share will go to the other named beneficiaries. If no other beneficiaries are named, the plan might name a default beneficiary, often the estate of the account owner.

A "shorthand" addition to the beneficiary designation can help resolve a potential family conflict. Add "per stirpes" after the beneficiary's name. "Per stirpes" means the beneficiary's share will go to the beneficiary's successor(s) should the beneficiary predecease the account owner.

Since beneficiary designations aren't reviewed very often, this is a very useful thing to know.

Avoid accidentally disinheriting your grandchildren. Add "per stirpes" to your beneficiary designations. For example, "John Smith, per stirpes." For more information and guidance, consult with legal counsel.

Conduit trusts – not as good anymore!

A conduit trust is a trust that requires that all distributions received by the trust from the decedent's retirement account must be paid to only one beneficiary and for which the trustee has no power to accumulate plan distributions in the trust. Qualification as a conduit trust hasn't changed under the SECURE Act.

Conduit trusts were widely used before 2020 when families wanted to preserve the maximum distribution period for an account without distributing the ownership of the account to the beneficiary immediately after the death of the participant.

Under the SECURE Act, the balance of an IRA held by a conduit trust inherited from a participant or an account beneficiary who is deceased after 2019 must be distributed within 10 years when a conduit trust beneficiary who is a child of the participant reaches majority (age 21). In many cases, that would be an economic disaster because the beneficiary might not be capable of managing a large distributed balance. For all other beneficiaries that aren't eligible designated beneficiaries, the account must be distributed within 10 years after the death of the participant.

A conduit trust eliminates some of the difficulties of other trusts that can accumulate distributions, or that have multiple beneficiaries. For example, a charity can't be a second-tier remainder beneficiary for a retirement account and still qualify for life expectancy distributions when the participant dies before the required beginning date unless the charity is a remainder beneficiary of a conduit trust that is the named beneficiary of the account.

Anyone who has a retirement account with a large balance that has a conduit trust beneficiary should immediately meet with an attorney to update their estate plan for the account. It may be a better estate plan to use a trust that isn't a conduit trust.

Conduit trusts still are especially useful for beneficiaries who are disabled or chronically ill, provided distributions won't reduce government benefits, such as Medi-Cal or disability Social Security.

When such a trust is the beneficiary of an IRA or Roth account, the required minimum distribution rules say that the beneficiary of the trust is considered to be the named beneficiary of the IRA or Roth account. The same rules apply for computing required minimum distributions for the trust as for the beneficiary of the trust.

The remainder beneficiaries of the conduit trust are disregarded when computing required minimum distributions.

In the case of a minor or an incompetent beneficiary, the payment of the passed through distributions from the IRA or Roth account can be made to the legal guardian of the minor or disabled beneficiary. The IRS has privately ruled that distributions for a beneficiary may be paid to a special needs trust.

The payment of trust administration expenses using retirement account funds doesn't disqualify the trust as a conduit trust.[43]

Grantor trusts

Certain trusts known as grantor trusts or revocable living trusts are disregarded for income tax purposes under the Internal Revenue Code during the lifetime of the trustor(s). The trust creator or beneficiary is treated for all income tax purposes as if that person was the owner of the trust's assets. During the participant's lifetime, such a trust can be structured to qualify after death as a beneficiary for single life expectancy distributions by designating subtrusts on the account beneficiary form. A qualified attorney can design such a trust.

Charitable beneficiaries

If the family has charitable inclinations and sufficient non-retirement assets to provide for the successors of the participant, charities are great candidates to be named beneficiaries. The charitable gift is deductible for estate tax purposes. The benefits paid to the charity escape income tax. A winning combination.

When the charity is one of multiple first-tier or second-tier beneficiaries of a trust, be sure to have the share of the charity in a retirement account either paid off or segregated from the shares of any individual beneficiaries before September 30 of the taxable year after the year the participant died.

A charity that is the named beneficiary for a retirement account is a non-designated beneficiary. When the plan participant dies before the required beginning date and there is no designated beneficiary, the account must be distributed by the fifth year after death. When the plan participant dies after the required beginning date, "ghost" required minimum distributions must be made based on the remaining life expectancy of the deceased

43 Letter Rulings 200432027, 200432029

participant, reduced by one for each subsequent year. *Remember that a charity that won't receive its inherited share until two other beneficiaries die isn't "counted" and the trust won't be subject to the five-year distribution requirement in that case.* I would think most charities would elect to distribute the account as soon as possible, since retirement account distributions aren't taxable income for charities.

A charitable beneficiary for which there is some ongoing flexibility for choosing the ultimate charity to receive the benefit is a donor advised fund. Persons you name can direct which charities will receive gifts from the donor advised fund. See your estate planning attorney for details.

Warning: Doing this through a trust is <u>very</u> hazardous, but possible.

In addition, in order for the trust to qualify for the income tax charitable deduction, the trust must require that the charitable gift be paid out of the trust's gross income. In most cases, the date of death balance in a Roth or IRA account will be principal, not income.

Charitable remainder trust

The benefits of a retirement account can be made payable to a charitable remainder trust (CRT). At the death of the participant, the IRA can be paid all at once to the CRT, eliminating the need for required minimum distributions. The annuity or unitrust payments can be paid to a special needs trust for a disabled beneficiary.[44] (The principal ultimately goes to a charity.)

A charitable remainder trust might help to mitigate the new ten-year distribution requirement under the SECURE Act. You should only use one of these when you have a charitable intent.

Inherited accounts

Beneficiaries of inherited retirement accounts usually should designate their own remainder beneficiaries, since the remainder beneficiary designations of the participant usually become ineffective once the beneficiary for the account is determined after the participant's death.

(Successor beneficiaries may be named by the account owner/participant when the IRA or Roth IRA account has a trustee custodian. Most account custodians aren't trustees. Successor beneficiaries may also be designated when a trust is the named beneficiary of the retirement account. See the planning issues for trusts above.)

For inherited accounts relating to the death of a participant before 2020, the single life factor for distributions is generally based on the single life expectancy of the beneficiary as of the date of death of the participant, reduced by one for each subsequent year.

See the discussions above and in Chapter 19 about required minimum distributions for inherited retirement accounts.

44 Revenue Ruling 2002-20

For accounts inherited from a beneficiary of a participant who was deceased before 2020 and the beneficiary was deceased after 2019, the account must generally be distributed by December 31 of the year that includes the 10th anniversary of the death of the previous beneficiary (that the account was inherited from). Annual required minimum distributions continue to be made from the inherited account based on the original beneficiary's remaining life expectancy schedule until the balance is distributed during the 10th year after the death of the previous beneficiary.

Planning adjustments under the SECURE Act and SECURE 2.0 Act

Estate planning for retirement accounts is harder under the SECURE Act, SECURE 2.0 Act and the final and proposed regulations. The most popular alternatives have lost many of their advantages. I don't have any magic solutions. Here are some suggestions to consider.

Worth worrying about? If the balances in the retirement accounts are relatively small, just having named beneficiaries is probably sufficient.

Should the surviving spouse be the sole beneficiary for the retirement accounts? The surviving spouse has the most flexibility for handling an inherited retirement account, including the ability to roll the account to their own account.

When the surviving spouse is the sole beneficiary for a retirement account that isn't rolled over to their own account, the balance at the surviving spouse's death will probably have to be distributed within ten years, resulting in a potential concentration of income and higher income tax bills. With the spouse's consent, perhaps there should be one or more retirement accounts with other beneficiaries. The spouse should have separate counsel when making this decision.

Lifetime Roth conversions. By converting taxable retirement accounts to Roth accounts over many years, the tax rates that apply to the conversion can possibly be reduced dramatically, when the account owner is not already subject to the highest income tax rates. Conversions can be done during market downswings to take advantage of lower valuations. Paying the income taxes for the conversion during your lifetime can reduce your taxable estate. Remember distributions aren't required from Roth accounts during the participant's lifetime, enabling the account to grow in value and distribution of the account to your beneficiaries will be income tax free.

Lifetime contributions to employer plan Roth accounts. In exchange for paying income taxes up front for non-deductible or taxable Roth contributions, you get a tax-free accumulation of earnings with no required distributions during your lifetime. Your beneficiaries receive an income tax free inheritance, with an additional ten-year distribution deferral if you die before your required beginning date. The younger you are, the more appealing Roth accounts are. The income tax payments that you make also reduce your potential taxable estate.

Reconsider conduit trusts for most beneficiaries who are not eligible designated beneficiaries. The requirement to distribute the account within ten years after reaching age 21 for beneficiaries who are children of the deceased plan participant probably defeats the purpose for many of these trusts. They still make sense for surviving spouses and beneficiaries who are disabled or chronically ill. Having a "switch" provision written in the trust to convert a conduit trust to an accumulation trust disqualifies the trust from being a conduit trust, including giving a trust protector the power to make the switch.

Multiple accounts/multiple beneficiaries? If retirement accounts are divided up among several beneficiaries, the income tax bill can be dramatically reduced. A $200,000 account divided by 20 children and grandchildren would be $10,000 each.

Should you plan for a big income tax bill? If taxable accounts aren't converted during lifetime to Roths, higher income taxes will likely have to be paid when an account is distributed within ten years after death. With the high federal budget deficits we are experiencing, higher income tax rates might be coming, despite the Trump administration plans to extend the tax cuts in the Tax Cuts and Jobs Act of 2017 that are scheduled to expire after 2025. Consider funding expected income tax liabilities, potential estate tax liabilities and lost benefits using life insurance held in irrevocable life insurance trusts.

Fund charitable bequests with retirement accounts. Charities don't pay income taxes. If you have charitable intentions and sufficient assets for your family, leave your retirement accounts to charities.

Consider the charitable remainder trust. Charitable remainder trusts can be a way to avoid income tax liabilities while funding a lifetime benefit. The problem is if the beneficiary of the trust dies prematurely, the balance goes to charity. Consider using life insurance with an irrevocable life insurance trust to fund other family beneficiaries in the event of that contingency. CRTs require actual charitable intent, requiring at least a 10 percent charitable interest, based on actuarial tables. There likely will be less value for the individual beneficiary compared to living with the 10-year rule.

Consider using an accumulation trust. We usually avoid accumulation trusts because they reach high income tax rates at the low taxable income threshold of $15,200 for 2024 and $15,650 for 2025. When the participant wants professional management of the funds when they are distributed within ten years after death, the accumulation trust is still a reasonable choice. Plan for the income taxes and any estate taxes for the retirement account distribution using life insurance.

Prepare the family, executor and trustee

The time frames for taking action for the retirement accounts after the death of the participant are short. There can be long-term consequences for any missteps. The estate planning team should brief the family, executor and trustees well in advance so they know what to do to assure the objectives of the family are accomplished.

The best planning is done when the IRA or Roth owner is still living. After death, the estate plan should be timely implemented.

19

Handling an IRA or Roth account after a death

The detailed rules for handling an IRA or Roth account after a death are complex and beyond the scope of this book. Seek advice from a legal or tax professional who knows the rules. A more detailed helpful reference is *Life and Death Planning for Retirement Benefits, 8th Edition* by Natalie Choate. It was released in 2019, before the SECURE Act, SECURE 2.0 Act and Final and Proposed Treasury Regulations implementing the SECURE Act and SECURE 2.0 Act. Natalie Choate generously makes extensive updates for developments available for free at www.ataxplan.com.

The time frame for many of the actions that are necessary can be very short, especially for a family that is grieving and may not be giving prompt attention to financial matters. The IRA plan administrators typically aren't proactive in getting the accounts settled (they might not know the account owner is deceased!) and the executor and trustee usually don't have authority to administer retirement accounts. That means the beneficiaries have to take action to preserve their benefits and assure the requirements are met. Hopefully they know the details for the accounts to claim their benefits and get professional advice to avoid making errors and paying taxes that could be postponed or avoided.

Some of the requirements for handling inherited retirement accounts have been changed by the SECURE Act of 2019 and SECURE 2.0 Act of 2022 and explained in final and proposed regulations issued by the IRS. I explain highlights of the changes in this chapter and Chapter 18.

See Chapter 16 for an explanation of the Required Beginning Date (RBD). Roth IRA accounts don't have a RBD. Effective for tax years beginning after December 31, 2023, Roth accounts in a 401(k) or other employer retirement plan Roth accounts also generally don't have a RBD. Before those tax years, Roth 401(k) accounts did have a RBD.

There is an exception for designated Roth accounts (DRACs) when the participant also owns a traditional (taxable) account in the same retirement plan. In that case, the RBD will be the same for the DRAC as for the traditional account, SOLELY for the purpose of determining whether RMDs are required after the death of the participant. (Lifetime distributions aren't required.)[45]

The requirements for distributions after death are quite different depending on whether the account owner is deceased before the RBD or on or after the RBD.

When using this list, be aware required minimum distributions are waived for RMDs that would have been due during 2020. The waiver was enacted as COVID-19 relief

45 Treasury regulations section 1.401(a)(9)-5(b)(3), proposed regulations sections 1.401(a)(9)-5(g)(2)(iii) and 1.402(c)-2(f)(3), SECURE 2.0 Act section 325

under the CARES Act of 2020. Although a payment was waived for a required beginning date during 2020, it will still be the required beginning date for other purposes, such as determining which distribution schedule applies. The 10-year limit and 5-year limit for the final distribution of retirement plans are unchanged when the date of death for the account owner was during 2020.[46]

The Proposed Treasury Regulations issued during 2022 implementing the SECURE Act of 2019 included some controversial provisions that were a surprise to tax and legal advisors. The IRS issued Notices 2022-53, 2023-54, and 2024-35 which announced the IRS waived penalties for failure to make required minimum distributions from certain inherited retirement accounts for 2021, 2022, 2023 and 2024, effectively waiving required minimum distributions (RMDs) for certain inherited accounts for those years. Amounts paid from those retirement accounts, up to the RMD amount, aren't eligible for a rollover. Previously undistributed RMDs for those years must be distributed before rolling over an account, for example, transferring an inherited 401(k) account to a beneficiary IRA account. Since a transfer from a traditional IRA account to a beneficiary account isn't a rollover, it might not be subject to this requirement.

The following "eligible designated beneficiaries" don't qualify for the waiver:

- surviving spouse,
- minor child of the deceased participant,
- a beneficiary who is disabled or chronically ill, and
- an individual who is none of those previously listed and who is not more than ten years younger than the deceased participant.

Those beneficiaries qualify for "life expectancy" distributions, starting with the year after the death of the participant. When one of those beneficiaries dies after December 31, 2019, the balance of the account must be distributed no later than the end of the year that includes the 10th anniversary of the beneficiary's date of death. The distribution for the year of death of the participant who died after the required beginning date also doesn't qualify for the waiver.

Final regulations implementing the SECURE Act of 2019 and some provisions of the SECURE 2.0 Act of 2022 and proposed regulations implementing other provisions of the SECURE 2.0 Act of 2022 were issued on July 19, 2024, mostly effective for tax years after 2024.

Effective for taxable years beginning after December 29, 2022, the penalty for failure to make a required minimum distribution is 25% of the undistributed amount and might be reduced to 10% if the participant timely receives a corrective distribution. Before 2023, the penalty was 50% of the undistributed amount. In addition to required payments on or after the required beginning date (see Chapter 16), penalties can apply for a series of substantially equal payments before age 59 ½ and for inherited retirement accounts. (The taxpayer can request that the IRS waive the penalties for a "reasonable cause".) Any formal change in the regulations would likely only apply to future years.

SECURE 2.0 Act of 2022 extends the Employee Plans Compliance Resolution System to IRAs and Roth IRAs, providing procedures to correct failures resulting in a penalty. See Chapter 7 for more details.

46 Notice 2020-51

Here are some tips for handling retirement accounts after a death.

1. Remember that the decedent's required minimum distribution for the year of death must be distributed to a beneficiary by December 31 of the year of death. (Avoid the penalty for not making a required minimum distribution, explained above.)

   If a spousal rollover is made before making the required minimum distribution, there could be two penalties: one for failing to make a required minimum distribution, a second for making an excess contribution to the account of the surviving spouse!

2. In most cases, the IRA is distributable to a named beneficiary, not as directed in a will or trust. If there is no named beneficiary, see the plan documents or IRA adoption agreement.

3. Watch spousal rollovers or converting accounts to the surviving spouse's name. If the surviving spouse is under age 59 ½, penalty-free death benefits can be paid from a survivor "inherited" account, but not from an account in the surviving spouse's name.[47] A surviving spouse who is the sole beneficiary of a deceased spouse's account can convert it to his or her own name any time later, but see items 5 and 6. If the account participant dies before the required beginning date (Chapter 16), the surviving spouse may elect for the ten-year rule to apply. That would benefit a surviving spouse whose age results in required minimum distributions over less than 10 years (age 81 or older).

   If the surviving spouse makes that election and takes no distributions during the first nine years after the death of the participant and then elects to roll the account into the surviving spouse's name, there is an anti-gaming provision that reduces a rollover made before the year the surviving spouse reaches the age for which required minimum distributions start for him or her. The rollover isn't allowed for the cumulative total of what would have been required minimum distributions that would have belonged to the surviving spouse during the delayed rollover period.[48]

   The surviving spouse can alternatively consult with a financial planner to determine his or her requirement to maintain his or her standard of living before age 59 ½, retain that amount in the inherited account until age 59 ½ and immediately roll any remaining funds to his or her own account.

4. Effective for surviving spouses whose RMDs from their deceased spouse's account began in *2023 or earlier*, a surviving spouse beneficiary of an inherited Roth or IRA account that isn't rolled over to his or her own account has required minimum distributions based on the single life table, with the divisor based on the life expectancy of the surviving spouse on the table each year. The ten-year distribution requirement doesn't apply to a surviving spouse. If the participant died on or after the required beginning date, life expectancy distributions for the surviving spouse will commence for the year after the death of the participant. If the participant died before the required beginning date, life expectancy distributions for the surviving spouse will begin the later of the year the deceased spouse would have reached

47 Internal Revenue Code Section 72(t)(2)(A)(ii)
48 Treasury Regulations Section 1.402(c)-2(j)(4)(ii)

applicable age for the required beginning date or the year following the year of death. See also items 3, 5 and 6.

5. A surviving spouse who is the sole beneficiary of an IRA (not as a sole beneficiary of a trust) may elect to treat the surviving spouse's entire interest in the deceased spouse's IRA as the surviving spouse's own IRA. The election may not be made after the later of (A) the calendar year in which the surviving spouse reaches the age for which required minimum distributions must commence; and (B) the calendar year following the calendar year of the deceased spouse's death. Failure to receive a required minimum distribution as the death beneficiary is treated as a spousal election to treat the IRA as an IRA of the surviving spouse.

6. Effective for calendar years beginning *after December 31, 2023*, when the participant spouse dies before their RBD, a surviving spouse beneficiary may elect to be treated as the deceased account owner for determining required minimum distributions. According to proposed regulations issued July 19, 2024, this election is automatically treated as being made. In Announcement 2025-2, the IRS announced the effective date for the Proposed Regulations issued July 19, 2024 won't be effective until 2026. As a precaution, the surviving spouse should actually make the election for 2024 and 2025. (It's unknown if an election-out can be done, but it usually wouldn't be to the advantage of the surviving spouse). The date on which distributions from the account are required to begin won't be earlier than the required beginning date when the account owner would have reached the applicable age for required minimum distributions. (See Chapter 16.) The RMDs for the surviving spouse are computed using the Uniform Lifetime Table for the surviving spouse's age (with recalculation), not the Single Life Table. (In the past, the surviving spouse was required to use the Single Life Table, with larger RMDs. See item 4.)

   The election isn't automatic when the account owner died on or after their RBD, but the election may be a default election under the plan.
   If the surviving spouse dies before distributions to the surviving spouse begin, the account is treated as inherited from the surviving spouse. The election isn't available to a beneficiary spouse of the surviving spouse.

   This election is important for a surviving spouse who is much younger than the account owner. Distributions from an inherited account are death benefits, not subject to the penalty for distributions before age 59 ½. Although the surviving spouse is treated as the owner of the account for computing distributions, the account is still considered an inherited account to avoid the early distribution penalty.

   If the surviving spouse remarries and names the new spouse as the beneficiary of the account, the new spouse won't qualify to roll over the inherited account to their own IRA. This is a disadvantage for a surviving spouse keeping an inherited account and not rolling it to the surviving spouse's own IRA. This proposed regulation is proposed to be effective for surviving spouse beneficiaries whose first RMD year would be 2024 or later, even if the deceased account owner died many years earlier.

For example, John died in 2015 at age 60, leaving his IRA to his wife, Jane. He would have reached his applicable age (73) in 2028. If Jane still held the account as an inherited IRA, she would start receiving RMDs no later than 12/31/2028 using the Uniform Lifetime Table.

Another disadvantage of keeping an inherited account is the RMD calculation for an employer account that includes a designated Roth account, or DRAC, *includes the DRAC account balance.*[49] Therefore, RMDs must be paid from a DRAC to a surviving spouse beneficiary. This is an incentive to roll the account to a beneficiary Roth IRA under the surviving spouse's name as soon as practical, because no distributions would then be required during the surviving spouse's lifetime.

The election to be treated as the deceased account owner for determining required minimum distributions does not apply for surviving spouses whose RMDs from their deceased spouse's account began in 2023 or earlier.

7. An inherited 401(k) can be converted to a Roth by direct transfer after death. An inherited IRA can't be converted to an inherited Roth IRA. (Crazy!)[50]

8. If a qualified terminable interest property (QTIP) election is made for a trust for the benefit of the surviving spouse which is named as the beneficiary of a retirement account, the election must be made for both the retirement account and the marital trust.[51] The QTIP election makes property that would otherwise be subject to federal estate tax eligible for the marital deduction on the deceased spouse's federal estate tax return. That property is included in the taxable estate of the surviving spouse. Both the retirement plan benefit and the trust must meet the marital deduction requirements, so the spouse must have the right to all of the trust's and the plan's income annually.

   Effective when the participant dies after 2019, when the QTIP trust isn't a conduit trust, the retirement account must be distributed to that trust by the end of the year in which the tenth anniversary of the participant's death falls. The QTIP trust does not qualify for the surviving spouse exemption from the ten-year distribution requirement. In that case, annual distributions aren't required, *except when the account owner died after the decedent's required beginning date*, thereby activating the "at least as rapidly" rule. That rule requires that, when the account owner died after the decedent's required beginning date, required distributions are computed for the first nine years after death using the greater of the life expectancy of the decedent or the surviving spouse. The balance of the account is distributed to the QTIP trust during the year that includes the tenth anniversary of the decedent's date of death. (See also, Chapter 18. The surviving spouse who is the primary beneficiary of a conduit trust that is the named beneficiary of a retirement account is also considered to be the beneficiary of the retirement account.)

   Effective when the decedent died before 2020, RMDs of a QTIP trust are paid based on the single life expectancy of the oldest beneficiary, usually the surviving spouse. If the QTIP trust qualifies as a conduit trust, the required minimum

49 Treasury Regulations Section 1.401(a)(9)-5(b)(3)

50 Treasury Regulations Section 1.408-A-10, A-7, Notice 2008-30, A-7. Internal Revenue Code Section 408(d)(3)(C)

51 Revenue Rulings 2006-26 and 2000-2

distribution should be computed based on the life expectancy of the surviving spouse, with annual recalculation. A conduit QTIP trust qualifies for the surviving spouse exemption from the ten-year distribution requirement. QTIP trusts must annually distribute the greater of the RMD for an IRA or the internal income of the IRA.

9. Remember that beneficiaries who aren't surviving spouses are required to take required minimum distributions from Roth accounts. (See an exception where surviving spouses who are beneficiaries of designated Roth accounts in employer plans must also take RMDs at item 6.) Since the participant was not required to take distributions during his or her lifetime, this is an easy item to miss.[52]

10. Effective for participants who are deceased after 2019, beneficiaries of Roth IRAs who are not surviving spouses or eligible designated beneficiaries are required to distribute the balance of the account by the end of the year that includes the tenth anniversary of the decedent's death. In that case, annual distributions aren't required, since Roth IRA owners have no Required Beginning Date. (See an exception where surviving spouses who are beneficiaries of designated Roth accounts in employer plans do have a required beginning date and must also take RMDs at item 6.)

11. Minor children of the deceased participant (not grandchildren or other descendants or other minor beneficiaries) are not subject to the ten-year distribution requirement until they reach majority at age 21. Starting for the year after the death of the participant, RMDs are computed based on the life expectancy of the beneficiary using the single life table for that year. After the initial year, one is subtracted from the divisor for the previous year. Life expectancy required minimum distributions continue until the balance of the account is distributed during the year the child reaches age 31. At that time the account must be distributed in full.

12. Effective for years after 2019, disabled beneficiaries and chronically ill beneficiaries are eligible designated beneficiaries who are not subject to the ten-year distribution rule. When the plan participant died on or after the required beginning date, RMDs are computed based on the greater of the life expectancy of the beneficiary or the deceased participant from the single life table for the year after death. When the plan participant died before the required beginning date, required distributions are computed based on the life expectancy of the beneficiary from the single life table for the year after death. After the initial year, one is subtracted annually from the divisor for the previous year. The life-expectancy distribution continues after the death of the disabled or chronically ill beneficiary, and the balance of the account is distributed during the year that includes the tenth anniversary of the beneficiary's date of death. When the plan participant died on or after the required beginning date, the balance of the account is distributed no later than the final year of the *beneficiary's* life expectancy determined for the year after the participant's date of death. *That date could be less than ten years after the participant's date of death!*

13. The final regulations provide rules for "Applicable Multi-Beneficiary Trusts", or AMBTs. The rules enable setting up trusts as "supplementary needs trusts"

52 Internal Revenue Code Section 408A(c)(5), Treasury Regulations Section 1.408A-6, A-14(b)

or "special needs trusts" for beneficiaries who are disabled or chronically ill. The beneficiaries who are disabled or chronically ill are the primary beneficiaries of the trust, and can only receive very limited benefits from the trust to protect government benefits, like Medicaid. The other beneficiaries of the trust can be individuals or certain qualified charities (not donor advised funds or supporting organizations), and can't receive distributions during the lifetime of the disabled or chronically ill beneficiary(ies).[53]

RMDs are payable to the trust and are computed based on the life expectancy of the oldest disabled or chronically ill beneficiary for the year after the death of the account owner with one subtracted for each subsequent year.

The balance of the account must be distributed during the year that includes the tenth anniversary of the death of the last disabled or chronically ill beneficiary.

14. When the deceased participant's date of death is after 2019 and before the required beginning date, the eligible designated beneficiaries, including the surviving spouse, minor children, and disabled and chronically ill beneficiaries, may elect to apply the ten-year distribution rule. In that case, no lifetime distributions are required until the year that includes the tenth anniversary of the participant's date of death.

The ten-year distribution rule would apply if:

- the applicable plan document requires it, or
- the participant directs it in the beneficiary designation form, or
- the eligible designated beneficiary elects it, and the election is permitted in the plan.

The election, if the plan permits it, can be made up to the end of the ninth year after the death of the participant. See item 3 about the interplay of this rule with rollovers by the surviving spouse.

15. Special rules apply when a trust is a beneficiary of a retirement account and the participant died before his or her required beginning date. The account might be distributable within five years after death unless the beneficiaries' lives are ascertainable (all "countable" beneficiaries are individuals) and other requirements are met.[54] It may be that adjustments need to be made, including making disclaimers or dividing accounts to separate beneficiaries. The deadline to have the accounts segregated and designated beneficiaries identified is September 30 of the year after the participant's death. The deadline for providing trust documentation for post-death distributions to the plan administrator is October 31 of the year after the participant's death.[55]

Under final regulations issued by the IRS to implement the SECURE Act for years after 2019, trusts with multiple tiers of beneficiaries may have a non-individual

---

53 Treasury Regulations Section 1.401(a)(9)-4(g)(1)
54 Treasury Regulations Section 1.401(a)(9)-3, A-2 & A-4
55 Treasury Regulations Section 1.401(a)(9)-4

beneficiary when that beneficiary is named after a first- and second-tier beneficiary and not be subject to the five-year distribution rule. Only the first two "tiers" of beneficiaries are "counted" for determining required minimum distributions. This new rule will make it easier for trusts with multiple beneficiaries to avoid the five-year distribution requirement.

16. If the participant died before his or her required beginning date and there was no designated beneficiary for the account (including having the estate as the beneficiary), the account must be distributed by December 31 of the year that contains the fifth anniversary of the participant's date of death. Under the five-year distribution rule, annual distributions aren't required.[56]

    Note that, since there is no required beginning date for a Roth IRA, the five-year rule and its exceptions will always apply if there is no designated beneficiary for a Roth IRA.[57]

17. For participants deceased after 2019, if there is a designated beneficiary for a Roth account who isn't an eligible designated beneficiary, the account balance must be distributed by December 31 of the year that includes the 10th anniversary of the participant's death and no annual distributions are required. For participants deceased before 2020, if there is a designated beneficiary for a Roth IRA, minimum required distributions apply to the designated beneficiary, based on his or her life expectancy.[58]

18. For beneficiaries who aren't surviving spouses or eligible designated beneficiaries, the account, including Roth and traditional IRAs, must be distributed by December 31 of the year that includes the tenth anniversary of the participant's death. No annual distributions are required, unless the participant died on or after the required beginning date. When the account owner died after the decedent's required beginning date, required distributions are computed for the first nine years after death using the greater of the life expectancy of the decedent or the designated beneficiary. The balance of the account is distributed to the designated beneficiary during the year that includes the tenth anniversary of the decedent's date of death.

19. When the participant was deceased before 2020, required minimum distributions (including from traditional IRAs and Roth IRAs) for trusts are computed using the life expectancy of the oldest beneficiary using the beneficiary's age on his or her birthday in the year after the year of the participant's death. The life expectancy is the divisor to determine the distribution for the year after the participant's death. Thereafter, one is annually subtracted from the previous year's divisor. If the participant was deceased after the required beginning date, the decedent's single life expectancy without recalculation can be used if it results in a longer distribution schedule.

    See items 3 through 6 about considerations for surviving spouses.

20. Nonspouse beneficiaries can't rollover inherited IRAs, Roths or retirement

56 Internal Revenue Code Section 401(a)(9)(B)(ii), Treasury Regulations Sections 1.401(a)(9)-3, A-2 and A-4

57 Internal Revenue Code Section 408A(c)(5)

58 Treasury Regulation Section 1.408A-6, A-14(b)

accounts to their own account, but can make a direct transfer to an "inherited" account, for which they are named as the beneficiary.[59] Making a direct transfer is critical, as there is no possibility to make a rollover.

21. Under the California Probate Code, only 10% of retirement plan distributions are allocated to income.[60] Since principal might not be distributable to an income beneficiary of the trust, this may result in part of the distribution being retained by the trust that is needed by the income beneficiaries and the distribution being taxed to the trust based on its compressed federal income rate schedule. (There can be family arguments about these payments.) This rule doesn't apply to QTIP trusts. (See the section on QTIP Trusts in the chapter on Estate Planning for IRAs and Roths.) Also, a lump sum payment under the "five-year" distribution rule for beneficiaries that aren't individuals is 100% principal.

22. As mentioned above, when the "five-year" or "ten-year" distribution requirements apply, annual distributions aren't required, unless the plan participant died after the required beginning date. Many beneficiaries will need distributions sooner for non-tax reasons, and there is no penalty for taking them sooner. The account just won't continue to grow as much. It may be advantageous to take distributions over two or more years, because of the reduced tax brackets at lower income levels. Also consider it seems likely that income rates will probably increase in the future, despite the Trump administration's intention to extend Federal income tax rates that are currently scheduled to increase after 2025, when the tax cuts in the Tax Cuts and Jobs Act of 2017 expire.) We suggest that you work with a financial planner and a tax consultant to make growth and tax projections to determine the best approach for your situation. With the uncertainty of the tax laws and the volatility of the financial markets, any conclusions will be an educated guess.

59 Internal Revenue Code Sections 402(c)(9), 408(d)(3)(C), 402(c)(11)(A)

60 California Probate Code Section 16361(c)

20
Divorce

Federal tax laws have been fashioned to enable divorcing spouses to separate their assets without incurring a tax liability.

Same sex married couples are now subject to the same rules as other married couples after the Supreme Court's rulings in *United States v. Windsor*[61] and *Obergefell v. Hodges.*[62]

Registered domestic partners don't currently qualify for this relief because their relationship isn't a marriage.

An error in handling a division of retirement accounts can be very costly. The tax may be accelerated and may apply to the participant spouse, not the recipient spouse. Penalties for early distributions can apply.

To avoid these consequences, the division should be handled by a skilled family law attorney, possibly together with a tax advisor who knows the rules in this area.

Qualified Plans

For qualified plan accounts, such as 401(k), profit sharing plans, and government and retirement plans of tax exempt entities, the account can be divided without tax or penalty using a Qualified Domestic Relations Order, or QDRO. The QDRO requirements are defined at Internal Revenue Code Sections 401(a)(13)(B) and 414(p).

A QDRO is a judgment, decree or order, including approval of a property settlement agreement made according to a state's domestic relations or community property law and relating to the provision of child support, alimony or marital property rights to a spouse, former spouse, child or other dependent of a plan participant, meeting certain form requirements. The QDRO must specify the number of payments or the period to which the order applies.

The IRS has provided sample language for a QDRO in Notice 97-11.

The QDRO is the documentation needed by the plan administrator to effect the division of the account.

Once the account is divided, the account received by the divorcing spouse is owned by him or her, and benefits can be based on his or her life expectancy, but the distribution for some qualified retirement plans may be based on the life expectancy of the plan participant.

There is an exception from the penalty for distributions before age 59 ½ when a divorcing spouse receives benefits under a QDRO, so a divorcing spouse can receive penalty-

61 *United States v. Windsor*, 2013-2 USTC ¶ 60,667, June 26, 2013

62 *Obergefell v. Hodges*, 2015-1 USTC ¶ 50,357, June 26, 2015

free distributions before age 59 ½.[63]

The terms of the plan may restrict when benefits can begin to a divorcing spouse. However, an order will qualify even though it provides that payments to the alternate payee may begin on or after the date on which the participant attains the earliest retirement age under the plan, whether or not the participant actually retires on that date.

If in-service distributions are permitted to the plan participant, the former spouse can receive in-service distributions to the same extent as the plan participant.

Distributions to a former spouse under a QDRO are taxable to the former spouse. Distributions to another person, such as a child or dependent, are taxable to the plan participant.

IRAs and Roth IRAs

Although the QDRO rules don't apply to IRAs and Roth IRAs, the transfer of these accounts to a spouse or former spouse under a divorce or separation agreement is nontaxable.[64]

For tax years before 2019, the rules for divorce or separation agreements are similar to those that apply for the alimony/spousal support deduction.[65] Since the alimony/spousal support deduction was repealed by the Tax Cuts and Jobs Act of 2017 (except under grandfathered agreements), Congress changed the reference for divorce and separation agreements to the subsection on divorce for the exclusion from sale of gain for a principal residence.[66]

The transferred account is considered to be the IRA or Roth IRA account of the transferee spouse, so the rules for required distributions for them will be the same as for the transferee's other accounts.

Unlike qualified retirement plans, there is no exception to the penalty for distributions before reaching age 59 ½ for an IRA received by a spouse or former spouse under a divorce or separation agreement. The transferee spouse may qualify to take penalty-free distributions under an alternative exception, such as a series of substantially equal periodic payments.[67]

Qualified longevity annuity contracts

Retroactively for contracts purchased or received in an exchange on or after July 2, 2014, the SECURE 2.0 Act includes provisions protecting a divorced spouse's survivor benefits in a qualified longevity annuity contract (see Chapter 16) in a QDRO or divorce or separation agreement. The former spouse may be treated as a surviving spouse under the contract.

63 Internal Revenue Code Section 72(t)(2)(C)
64 Internal Revenue Code Section 408(d)(6)
65 Internal Revenue Code Section 71(b)(2)
66 Internal Revenue Code Section 121(d)(3)(C)(i)
67 Internal Revenue Code Section 72(t)(2)(A)(iv)

21

Additional references

IRS forms and instructions (available at www.irs.gov)

Form 990-T – Exempt Organization Business Income Tax Return

Form 990-W – Estimated Tax on Unrelated Business Taxable Income for Tax-Exempt Organizations

Form 1099R - Distributions From Pensions, Annuities, Retirement or Profit-Sharing Plans, IRAs, Insurance
Contracts, etc

Form 5305-A-SEP – Salary Reduction and Other Elective Simplified Employee Pension – Individual Retirement Accounts Contribution Agreement

Form 5305-SEP – Simplified Employee Pension – Individual Retirement Accounts Contribution Agreement

Form 5329 – Additional taxes on Qualified Plans (including IRAs) and Other Tax-Favored Accounts

Form 5330 – Return of Excise Taxes Relating to Employee Benefit Plans (excise tax on prohibited transactions)

Form 5500 Instructions (form may only be efiled) – Annual Return/Report of Employee Benefit Plan

Form 5500EZ – Annual Return of One Person (Owners and their Spouses) Retirement Plan

Form 5500SF Instructions (form may only be efiled) – Short Form Annual Return/Report of Small Employee Benefit Plan

Form 8606 – Nondeductible IRAs

Form 8880 – Credit for Qualified Retirement Savings Contributions

IRS Publications

Publication 560 – Retirement Plans For Small Businesses (SEP, SIMPLE and Qualified Plans)

Publication 575 – Pension and Annuity Income

Publication 590-A – Contributions to Individual Retirement Arrangements (IRAs)

Publication 590-B – Distributions from Individual Retirement Arrangements (IRAs)

Publication 598 – Tax On Unrelated Business Income of Exempt Organizations

Publication 4333 – SEP Retirement Plans For Small Businesses

Publication 4334 – SIMPLE IRA Plans for Small Businesses

Publication 4587 – Payroll Deduction IRAs For Small Businesses

Publication 4703 – Retirement Savings Contributions Credit

Books

The 2024 Pension Answer Book by Stephen J. Krass, Esq., Wolters Kluwer Law & Business

Life and Death Planning for Retirement Benefits, 8th Edition by Natalie Choate, Ataxplan Publications (Natalie Choate has written excellent updates relating to tax planning and estate planning for retirement accounts. You can get them for FREE at www.ataxplan.com.

2024 U.S. Master Pension Guide, by Kathleen Kelly Luzak et. al., Wolters Kluwer Law & Business

The Retirement Savings Time Bomb Ticks Louder by Ed Slott, Penguin Books

Television interviews about IRAs, Roth IRAs and retirement accounts

You can find FREE video interviews that have been posted on YouTube on a host of financial topics at www.financialinsiderweekly.com. Please be aware there have been significant developments after these interviews were recorded. They can be useful as a starting point for a conversation with your tax, financial and legal advisors.

Interviews especially related to IRAs, Roth IRAs and retirement accounts include:

Bill Neville of Entrust Administration – "Investing in real estate using your IRA or Roth account," and "Making alternative investments besides real estate using your IRA or Roth account"

Lamarr Baxter of Entrust Administration – "Investing in real estate using your IRA or Roth account," and "Making alternative investments besides real estate using your IRA or Roth account"

Tom Anderson, President of The Retirement Industry Trust Association and founder and former President of Pensco Trust – "Investing in real estate using your IRA or Roth account," and "Making alternative investments besides real estate using your IRA or Roth account"

Michael Jones, CPA, Thompson Jones LLP – "Beneficiary designations for retirement accounts," "Community property issues for retirement accounts," and "Handling retirement accounts after a death"

Jeffrey B. Hare, attorney – "Using a checkbook LLC to invest IRA and Roth funds"

Naomi Comfort, attorney, The Silicon Valley Elder Law Group, PC – "How to handle retirement accounts after a death"

Raymond Sheffield, attorney – "Estate planning for retirement accounts," and "Handling retirement accounts after a death"

Phil Price, EA, The Price Company – "Qualified retirement plans for small businesses"

22
About the Authors

Michael C. Gray founded his CPA firm, Michael Gray, CPA on October 1, 1996 and sold the firm to Thi T. Nguyen, CPA effective January 1, 2018. He has continuously worked in public accounting since June 1974. Mike was a co-founder and partner in charge of tax services of Hubler, Gray and Associates from June 1986 through September 1996 and a tax manager at KMG Main Hurdman, subsequently acquired by KPMG Peat Marwick, from February 1978 to June 1986.

The areas of practice that Mike has focused on include tax planning for individuals, estate and trust planning and administration, tax planning for businesses, tax examinations, and tax procedure. He also assists other tax practitioners in dealing with complex tax issues.

Mike was also the host of a weekly television show, called *Financial Insider Weekly.* You can find back episodes on YouTube.com at the channel, financialinsiderweek.

Mike has given many presentations and written many articles on tax subjects, including for the California Society of CPAs, Silicon Valley Bar Association and Santa Clara County Bar Association.

Mike has been a CPA in California since March 1977. He received his BS in accounting and MBA at San Jose State University in June 1974 and June 1978, respectively. He is a past president of the Silicon Valley San Jose chapter of the California Society for Certified Public Accountants (CalCPA), past chairman of the tax committee for that chapter and past member of the state tax committee for CalCPA. He received the Distinguished Achievement Award from the Silicon Valley San Jose chapter of CalCPA. He is also a past member of the Santa Clara County Estate Planning Council, and has been involved with the Executive Planning Committee of the Tax Section for the Santa Clara County Bar Association, and is a past lay member of the Silicon Valley Bar Association.

Michael Gray and his daughter and webmaster, Dawn Siemer, maintain several websites, including www.taxtrimmers.com, www.profitadvisors.com, www.stockoptionadvisors.com, www.realestateinvestingtax.com, www.tinyurl.com/busalchemy.com, and michaelgraycpa.com.

An article about the initial web site for Michael Gray, CPA appeared in the October 1997 *Journal of Accountancy.* KNTV News also featured a story on his web site in the Technology section of the Six O'Clock News, and he has been profiled in *The San Jose Mercury News.* Mike has been quoted in *The San Jose Mercury News, The San Francisco Chronicle, The Wall Street Journal,* and *The New York Times.*

He is the author of the *Real Estate Tax Handbook, Secrets of Tax Planning for Employee Stock Options, Employee Stock Options – Executive Tax Planning,* and co-author of *Employee Stock Options – A Strategic Planning Guide For The 21st Century Optionaire.*

Mike's personal interests include the study of martial arts. He received his black belt from West Coast Tae Kwon Do in May 1996. He has also studied American Kenpo and Aikido.

Mike appeared as a member of the cast of *South Pacific* with the West Valley Light Opera, which was performed during November and early December 1997. He received a director's award, called the Captain's Cape, as the outstanding chorus member. He also appeared in the West Valley Light Opera production of *Carousel* during October and November 1998 and was the voice of Florenz Ziegfeld in the West Valley Light Opera production of *Will Rogers Follies* during June and July 2000.

Ms. Thi T. Nguyen, CPA is a partner with ATL CPAs & Advisors, Inc. in San Jose since 2022. She previously was a principal with Koehler & Associates CPAs, Inc. in San Jose, where she was in charge of the tax practice. She joined Koehler & Associates in 2010, after working with Michael Gray, CPA for 10 years. Thi received a masters in taxation degree from San Jose State University and also bachelor's degrees in accounting and management information systems.

Thi is married to Allen Le, who is also a CPA and partner with ATL CPAs & Advisors, Inc. They have a son, Lance, and live in San Jose. They enjoy spending quality time with family and friends, and travel frequently to Vietnam to visit their extended family. Thi's hobbies include travel, listening to music and watching romances and comedies.

Appendix A
Retirement Plan Calendar checklist for after a plan participant's or Roth or IRA owner's death

Remember to read the plan. Its provisions override the possibilities of the tax law. For example, some plans require lump sum distributions or distribution of the balance of the account 10 years after the death of the account owner. Some plans specify the spouse as the "default" beneficiary when none is named while others may specify the estate.

Note relating to the following discussion: required minimum distributions were suspended for 2020 under the CARES Act as a COVID-19 relief measure. Despite the distribution being suspended, the required beginning date (RBD) is still used for other purposes.

In addition, the IRS has waived penalties for failing to make a required minimum distribution (RMD) from some retirement accounts inherited by individuals after the required beginning date for 2021, 2022, 2023 and 2024.[68] However, any "missed" required minimum distributions plus related earning for those years will have to be made before the balance of the account can be rolled over to an inherited IRA account.

The following "eligible designated beneficiaries" don't qualify for the waiver: surviving spouse, minor child of the deceased participant, a beneficiary who is disabled or chronically ill, and an individual who is none of those previously listed and who is not more than ten years younger than the deceased participant. Those beneficiaries qualify for "life expectancy" distributions, starting with the year after the death of the participant. See the next paragraph for an exception for the surviving spouse. The distribution for the year of death of the participant who died after the required beginning date also doesn't qualify for the waiver.

Effective for a surviving spouse who is the sole beneficiary for a retirement account and whose first RMD year is 2024 or later (the account owner was born in 1951 or later), when the account owner died before his or her required beginning date (RBD, April 1 of the year after he or she reached age 73 for 2024, see Chapter 16), RMDs begin the year the account owner would have reached his or her applicable age. If the account owner died on or after his or her RBD, RMDs begin the year after the death of the account owner. RMDs are computed using the Uniform Lifetime Table, based on the age of the surviving spouse, recalculated each year.

A surviving spouse who is under age 59 ½ might prefer to initially receive the account as a beneficiary account, because distributions from an inherited account aren't subject to the penalty for early distributions and the surviving spouse might need those funds. The account

68 Notices 2022-53, 2023-54, and 2024-35

can be rolled over to the surviving spouse's own account after reaching age 59 ½ to be able to delay taking more distributions until he or she reaches his or her own required beginning date. Also, if the surviving spouse remarries, the account must be in his or her own name for the "new" surviving spouse to qualify for the same sole surviving spouse benefits.

A Roth IRA is always received before the RBD, and RMDs apply for inherited Roth accounts when the surviving spouse is the sole beneficiary, so the surviving spouse should consider rolling the inherited Roth IRA to his or her own account to eliminate the requirement to take RMDs.

When an employer plan (like a 401(k) plan) includes both traditional (taxable) and designated Roth (DRAC) (tax-free) subaccounts, the DRAC is considered have a RBD for this purpose, so RMDs are required after death, with the balance generally payable during the year containing the 10th anniversary of the date of death. There are no annual distributions for most other Roth accounts. The exceptions for eligible designated beneficiaries apply.

See Chapters 18 and 19 about exceptions.

This checklist is not a substitute for getting tax and legal advice after a death. Get professional help before taking any significant actions.

<u>By the end of the year of death</u>

- If decedent-participant died after the required beginning date (see Chapter 16), a required minimum distribution must have been made to the decedent or successor beneficiary(s) for the account. (See above for an exception for a surviving spouse.)

- If the decedent was taking payments as a series of substantially equal periodic payments, a required minimum distribution must have been made to the decedent or successor beneficiary(s) for the account.

<u>By nine months after death</u>

- Qualified disclaimers must be done so that the status of beneficiaries as of September 30 of the year following the year of death can be established.

- Planned status and details of accounts (balance, community v. separate property, qualifying for marital or charitable deduction) must be determined to make a preliminary computation of estate tax to prepare estate tax returns or request for extension of time to file estate tax returns. Payment or application of extension of time for payment of estate tax is due.

- If multiple named beneficiaries (not of a trust) desire separate treatment, such as some wanting to cash out but others don't, their shares should be segregated into separate accounts by this date.

- Make a QTIP election for qualifying retirement accounts and QTIP trusts, which may be named beneficiaries of retirement accounts. (When applicable, the election must be made for both of them.)

By September 30 of the year following the year of death

- If the account is to be distributed over an extended period of time (more than five years), the interests of any "countable" disqualifying beneficiaries, including charities, disqualifying trusts, or the decedent-participant's estate should be eliminated by distributing their interest or disclaimer. Note that beneficiaries who would receive the inherited account only after two other beneficiaries died aren't "counted".

- Designated beneficiary(s) for the account(s) must be established.

- Once designated beneficiaries are established, they should consider establishing successor beneficiaries in the event of their death, if the plan permits it.

- If the surviving spouse is to be established as the sole designated beneficiary, other beneficiaries should be eliminated by segregating accounts, disclaimer or distribution.

By October 31 of the year following the year of death

- Required trust information must be provided to the administrator of the plan or IRA.

By December 31 of the year following the year of death

- Sole beneficiary surviving spouse can avoid having to receive required minimum distributions if the spouse rolls over or converts the account to his or her own name by December 31 of the year following the year of death.

- When the participant died after the required beginning date, required minimum distributions must be paid. See Chapters 18 and 19.

- Required minimum distributions must be paid to eligible designated beneficiaries. See above for an exception for certain surviving spouse sole beneficiaries.

- For IRA accounts with multiple (qualifying) designated beneficiaries that have been established by September 30 of the year following the year of death, and the participant died after the required beginning date, consider segregating into separate accounts for each beneficiary permitting separate decisions for distributing more than required minimum distributions. See Chapters 18 and 19.

Tax return for the year following the year of death

- If the participant died before the required beginning date and the plan permits it, the beneficiary may elect to apply the 10-year rule, permitting distributions to be postponed until the tenth year after death.

By December 31 of the calendar year that includes the fifth anniversary of the decedent's death.

- If decedent died before the required beginning date and there are no qualified beneficiaries (such as when the beneficiary is a charity, estate, or non-qualifying trust) or the beneficiary(s) elects to not receive benefits based on life expectancy, the entire account balance must be distributed by this date. When the participant died before 2020, or the beneficiary could have used the ten-year rule when the participant died after 2019, the beneficiary may elect to distribute the entire account balance by this date.

- Roth IRAs don't have a required beginning date, so the five-year rule will always apply to them if there are no qualified designated beneficiaries.

By December 31 of the year before a sole beneficiary spouse first reaches the applicable age for the required beginning date (Chapter 16)

- If the spouse has been receiving distributions as death benefits from an account in the deceased participant's name, consider rolling over the account or converting it to the surviving spouse's name to qualify for an extended distribution period using the Uniform Lifetime Table.

By April 1 of the year following the year a sole beneficiary spouse first reaches the applicable age for required minimum distributions (see Chapter 16.)

- If the spouse elected to convert the account or rolled it over to an account in his or her name, the required minimum distribution for the year the spouse first reached applicable age for required minimum distributions (see Chapter 16) must be made by this date. Two minimum distribution payments might have to be completed by the end of the year.

By December 31 of the calendar year including the ninth anniversary of the decedent's death

- If the spouse didn't convert the account or roll it over to an account in his or her name and elected to be subject to the 10-year rule, the surviving spouse should do the conversion or rollover to avoid an anti-gaming provision requiring that the rollover be reduced by a deemed required minimum distribution amount, being the cumulative total of what would have been required minimum distributions if the account had belonged to the spouse during the delayed rollover period.

By December 31 of the calendar year including the later of the tenth anniversary of the decedent's death or the tenth anniversary of the date that children of the participant reach age 21after the participant's death.

- For participants who died after 2019, beneficiaries, including trusts that weren't subject to the five-year distribution requirement or that don't qualify as eligible designated beneficiaries, must receive the balance of the account by this date. Annual distributions aren't required unless the participant died after the required beginning date. This deadline and any required minimum distributions also apply to successor beneficiaries of the account.

- When minor children of the deceased participant reach age 21, they are no longer eligible designated beneficiaries. The balance of the account must be distributed by December 31 of the year they reach age 31. There is an exception when the minor beneficiary dies before reaching age 21. See below for death of an eligible designated beneficiary.

<u>When a beneficiary dies after 2019 who inherited a retirement account before 2020.</u>

- Required minimum distributions continue for the first nine years after the death of the previous beneficiary using the same life expectancy computations as that beneficiary was using. The account must be distributed by December 31 of the year that includes the tenth anniversary of the beneficiary's death. That deadline will also apply for any other successor beneficiaries.

<u>Ten years after the death of an eligible designated beneficiary</u>

- When an eligible designated beneficiary dies, required minimum distributions continue on the same life expectancy schedule as during their lifetime, with the balance of the account distributed by December 31 of the year that includes the tenth anniversary of the eligible beneficiary's date of death.

- This rule also applies when the youngest child dies who is a beneficiary of a multiple-beneficiary trust and all of the beneficiaries were children of the participant.

<u>End of life expectancy for elderly eligible designated beneficiaries when the participant died after the RBD</u>

- The balance of the retirement account must be distributed no later than the end of the actuarial life of a beneficiary determined using the single life table for the beneficiary for the year after death, even though the beneficiary was able to take required minimum distributions based on the participant's life expectancy. When the beneficiary is older than the participant (who was older than the applicable age for the required beginning date), it's likely that life expectancy *will be less than ten years!*

Appendix B
IRS Actuarial Tables for Distributions

SINGLE LIFE TABLE – After 2021

Age	Life Expectancy	Age	Life Expectancy	Age	Life Expectancy	Age	Life Expectancy
0	84.6	30	55.3	60	27.1	90	5.7
1	83.7	31	54.4	61	26.2	91	5.3
2	82.8	32	53.4	62	25.4	92	4.9
3	81.8	33	52.5	63	24.5	93	4.6
4	80.8	34	51.5	64	23.7	94	4.3
5	79.8	35	50.5	65	22.9	95	4.0
6	78.8	36	49.6	66	22.0	96	3.7
7	77.9	37	48.6	67	21.2	97	3.4
8	76.9	38	47.7	68	20.4	98	3.2
9	75.9	39	46.7	69	19.6	99	3.0
10	74.9	40	45.7	70	18.8	100	2.8
11	73.9	41	44.8	71	18.0	101	2.6
12	72.9	42	43.8	72	17.2	102	2.5
13	71.9	43	42.9	73	16.4	103	2.3
14	70.9	44	41.9	74	15.6	104	2.2
15	69.9	45	41.0	75	14.8	105	2.1
16	69.0	46	40.0	76	14.1	106	2.1
17	68.0	47	39.0	77	13.3	107	2.1
18	67.0	48	38.1	78	12.6	108	2.0
19	66.0	49	37.1	79	11.9	109	2.0
20	65.0	50	36.2	80	11.2	110	2.0
21	64.1	51	35.3	81	10.5	111	2.0
22	63.1	52	34.3	82	9.9	112	2.0
23	62.1	53	33.4	83	9.3	113	1.9
24	61.1	54	32.5	84	8.7	114	1.9
25	60.2	55	31.6	85	8.1	115	1.8
26	59.2	56	30.6	86	7.6	116	1.8
27	58.2	57	29.8	87	7.1	117	1.6
28	57.3	58	28.9	88	6.6	118	1.4
29	56.3	59	28.0	89	6.1	119	1.1
						120+	1.0

UNIFORM LIFETIME TABLE – After 2021

Age of employee	Distribution period	Age of employee	Distribution period	Age of employee	Distribution period
10	88.2	47	51.5	84	16.8
11	87.2	48	50.5	85	16.0
12	86.2	49	49.5	86	15.2
13	85.2	50	48.5	87	14.4
14	84.2	51	47.5	88	13.7
15	83.2	52	46.5	89	12.9
16	82.2	53	45.6	90	12.2
17	81.2	54	44.6	91	11.5
18	80.2	55	43.6	92	10.8
19	79.2	56	42.6	93	10.1
20	78.2	57	41.6	94	9.5
21	77.2	58	40.7	95	8.9
22	76.2	59	39.7	96	8.4
23	75.2	60	38.7	97	7.8
24	74.2	61	37.7	98	7.3
25	73.3	62	36.8	99	6.8
26	72.3	63	35.8	100	6.4
27	71.3	64	34.9	101	6.0
28	70.3	65	33.9	102	5.6
29	69.3	66	33.0	103	5.2
30	68.3	67	32.0	104	4.9
31	67.3	68	31.1	105	4.6
32	66.3	69	30.1	106	4.3
33	65.3	70	29.2	107	4.1
34	64.3	71	28.3	108	3.9
35	63.3	72	27.4	109	3.7
36	62.3	73	26.5	110	3.5
37	61.3	74	25.5	111	3.4
38	60.3	75	24.6	112	3.3
39	59.4	76	23.7	113	3.1
40	58.4	77	22.9	114	3.0
41	57.4	78	22.0	115	2.9
42	56.4	79	21.1	116	2.8
43	55.4	80	20.2	117	2.7
44	54.4	81	19.4	118	2.5
45	53.4	82	18.5	119	2.3
46	52.4	83	17.7	120+	2.0

SINGLE LIFE TABLE – Before 2022

Age	Life Expectancy	Age	Life Expectancy	Age	Life Expectancy	Age	Life Expectancy
0	82.4	29	54.3	58	27.0	87	6.7
1	81.6	30	53.3	59	26.1	88	6.3
2	80.6	31	52.4	60	25.2	89	5.9
3	79.7	32	51.4	61	24.4	90	5.5
4	78.7	33	50.4	62	23.5	91	5.2
5	77.7	34	49.4	63	22.7	92	4.9
6	76.7	35	48.5	64	21.8	93	4.6
7	75.8	36	47.5	65	21.0	94	4.3
8	74.8	37	46.5	66	20.2	95	4.1
9	73.8	38	45.6	67	19.4	96	3.8
10	72.8	39	44.6	68	18.6	97	3.6
11	71.8	40	43.6	69	17.8	98	3.4
12	70.8	41	42.7	70	17.0	99	3.1
13	69.9	42	41.7	71	16.3	100	2.9
14	68.9	43	40.7	72	15.5	101	2.7
15	67.9	44	39.8	73	14.8	102	2.5
16	66.9	45	38.8	74	14.1	103	2.3
17	66.0	46	37.9	75	13.4	104	2.1
18	65.0	47	37.0	76	12.7	105	1.9
19	64.0	48	36.0	77	12.1	106	1.7
20	63.0	49	35.1	78	11.4	107	1.5
21	62.1	50	34.2	79	10.8	108	1.4
22	61.1	51	33.3	80	10.2	109	1.2
23	60.1	52	32.3	81	9.7	110	1.1
24	59.1	53	31.4	82	9.1	111+	1.0
25	58.2	54	30.5	83	8.6		
26	57.2	55	29.6	84	8.1		
27	56.2	56	28.7	85	7.6		
28	55.3	57	27.9	86	7.1		

UNIFORM LIFETIME TABLE – Before 2022

Age of employee	Distribution period	Age of employee	Distribution period
70	27.4	94	9.1
71	26.5	95	8.6
72	25.6	96	8.1
73	24.7	97	7.6
74	23.8	98	7.1
75	22.9	99	6.7
76	22.0	100	5.9
77	21.2	102	5.5
78	20.3	103	5.2
79	19.5	104	4.9
80	18.7	105	4.5
81	17.9	106	4.2
82	17.1	107	3.9
83	16.3	108	3.7
84	15.5	109	3.4
85	14.8	110	3.1
86	14.1	111	2.9
87	13.4	112	2.6
88	12.7	113	2.4
89	12.0	114	2.1
90	11.4	115+	1.9
91	10.8		
92	10.2		
93	9.6		

Joint and last survivor expectancy table when one spouse is more than 10 calendar years younger than the other

See Appendix C of Publication 590-B. You can get it at www.irs.gov. The table is too big to print here.

Made in United States
Orlando, FL
04 November 2026

90200290R00066